SEWING
AS A
HOME BUSINESS

MARY A. ROEHR

Dedicated with love and gratitude
to my father,
Mike Kalosh, Jr.

Mary Roehr Books & Video
500 Saddlerock Circle
Sedona, AZ 86336
520-282-4971

ISBN 0-9619229-2-3
Printed in U.S.A.

TABLE OF CONTENTS

DRESSMAKER

SEWING AS A
HOME BUSINESS

Sewing as a home business can be one of the easiest and most rewarding businesses there is to establish and operate. Since everyone wears clothes, there will be a limitless built-in source of income in any community, whether it be rural or metropolitan. There is also and will continue to be an expanding need for sewing-related services such as home dec, crafts, accessories, quilting, and many, many more.

Operating a home sewing business is perfect for people who want to stay home with their children or who are burnt out and in need of a career change. Many are planning a sewing related business as a supplement to retirement or as a new career after retirement. Others with physical limitations such as a handicap, a medical or dietary restriction, or being a day or night person find it ideal. Students can use it as a means of suppport while going to school.

A home sewing business can open an avenue of independence and creativity which is not possible in many other professions. You will have the flexibility and opportunity to develop your particular talents. You can specialize by choosing the work you want to do. You will not only be able to select the time of day you work, but you will also be able to select how much you work. It may be full time, more than full time, or part time. For some it could be a source of income in addition to a regular nine-to-five job.

A very big advantage to starting this type of business is that you will have to make virtually no investment. You can begin with the equipment you already have. Usually a sewing machine and an iron will be sufficient. As far as space goes, all that is needed at first is a small room or a corner of a room. Since your office is in your home, you will not have to spend extra money on rent or mortagage.

Probably the biggest advantage of having your own business is that you will be your own boss. You will be able to create a pleasant working environment for yourself without interference. You will make your own schedule, come and go as you please, and have the freedom to steer the business in whatever direction you choose.

Probably the biggest disadvantage is that it can be difficult to stop working or to leave your work behind at the end of the day. Having a separate room or a work area that can be completely closed off will help immensely.

A home sewing business is not for people who dislike being alone or who have trouble being self-motivated. You can however combat isolation and inactivity by taking classes and workshops, becoming involved in professional and social groups or clubs, and by subscribing to magazines and newspapers which pertain to your work.

You will be solely responsible for any mistakes, but you can take full credit for all your successes. As a result, you will develop a sense self-reliance and fulfillment. You will be providing a valuable service for which people are willing to pay. This will give you prestige and make you an asset to your community.

This book is a culmination of more than 20 years of research and experience. I know it will save you years of stress and grief and help to give you the confidence to succeed in whatever sewing endeavor you choose.

WHO WILL YOUR CUSTOMERS BE?

Target Markets, Advertising, and Promotion

In order to be effective in your business, you will need to decide who your customers will be. In other words, you need to choose your target market or target markets. By having more than one target market, you will be able to serve more people because you will have greater flexibility in your business. For instance, instead of doing only custom sewing, you could also do alterations, or instead of doing only window treatments, you could also make pillows or other home dec items.

Within the area sewing-related businesses, there are countless possibilities for target markets. A sampling is listed below.

ALTERATIONS
CUSTOM SEWING
MONOGRAMMING
COVERED BUTTONS & BELTS
COSTUMES
UNIFORMS
HALF SIZES
PETITES
TALLS
EMBELLISHMENT
SPORTSWEAR
SMOCKING
BABY CLOTHES
CAREER DRESSING
FLAGS OR BANNERS
QUILTING
PANTS
RESTYLING
SAMPLE MAKER
LEATHER
HOME DEC
UPHOLSTERY
BRIDALWEAR
MENDING

CRAFTS
PATCHWORK
DOLL CLOTHES
RESTYLING
PANTS
SQUARE DANCE
FORMALWEAR
SKIWEAR
FUR
SHIRTMAKING
CHILDREN'S CLOTHES
PUPPETS
FABRIC SCULPTURE
DRAPERIES
CUSTOM TAILORING
DESIGNING
MILLINERY
SILKSCREENING
TEACHING SEWING
CONTRACT SEWING
CONSIGNMENT
WESTERN WEAR
HEIRLOOM SEWING
KNITTING or CROCHETING

When selecting your target market or markets, you can do so on the basis of three things. First, the skills that you possess should play a large part. You can make a list of your particular aptitudes and then decide in which ones you are the most proficient.

Also, your desire to do a certain type of work is very important. For instance, you may aspire to sew for the handicapped, but you are only experienced in making clothing for your family. Because of your desire to reach your goal, you can draw upon the general sewing skills you already have and expand into your new area of interest through classes, research, and hands-on practice.

Thirdly, try to determine if there is a need for the service or product you would like to offer. Check newspapers, magazines, and the phone book in your area to see if anyone is already offering your idea. Talk to as many people as you can and consider their responses. Sometimes there may seem to be a proliferation of services or products similar to the ones you have chosen, but the quality is low. If you indeed can offer a better mousetrap, you can succeed.

Advertising and Promotion

Anyone can start a business, but not everyone can stay in business. You have chosen your target markets, laid the groundwork for your business, and now you need to let everyone know about it by deciding how to advertise and promote it. This will give your business direction and developing a plan of action will enhance your position should you apply for financing in the future.

Do everything from the beginning to promote yourself as a professional and people will naturally take you and your business seriously. In the sewing field, this will mean dressing and looking the part, on the job and off. It will also mean educating customers regarding the value of your service.

For anyone just starting out, the easiest, cheapest, and most effective way to promote your business is to get business cards. This will give customers something concrete to see and it provides a way for them to contact you later. Your name and phone number will be the most important information to convey. Some businesses do not include their addresses but print, "By Appointment Only" in order to discourage drop-ins. You may also add a motto, slogan, picture, or other artwork. Your cards can be as simple or as elaborate as your budget allows, and always give people two cards, one for them and one for a friend. As your business expands, a letterhead and stationery in the same design will add greatly to your overall image.

Advertising in the yellow pages is a good way to reach many people because this is the first place many prospective customers will look for a product or service they need. Here again, you must decide whether to print your address and if you are set up to handle walk-in clientele. Depending on your budget, you can also have a display ad in addition to your regular listing. This will distinguish you from a long list of names and numbers.

If you decide to run an ad in the newspaper, you will be paying for recognizability and credibility. It is important to realize that an ad should run at least six times to be effective. This is because the eye will pass over written material that it is not trying to perceive several times before noticing it.

Because of this, it is advisable to keep your ad simple, noticeable, and distinctive. The ad will need to have individuality so potential customers will recognize it. It will need to have clarity, which is the quality that enables readers to grasp the meaning, and it must appear continuously.

Direct mail is another way to get the word out to prospective customers. You can offer a coupon or special sale or simply tell about yourself and your product or service. You can begin mailing to friends and acquaintances. Lists from clubs and organizations are another good source for names. Mailing lists can also be purchased which will contain names of certain socio-economic groups or addresses for a certain geographical area. Look in the yellow pages under "mailing lists." Ten percent is considered a good return on direct mail, however you could probably expect a higher return if you were mailing to repeat customers. If you are planning to establish a customer list and/or do regular mailings, consult your postmaster about getting a bulk mailing permit. You will have to presort and bundle corrrespondence by zip codes, but the savings can be substantial.

If you are an outgoing and aggressive person, you may choose to promote your business through phone solicitations and direct sales. Phone solicitations should be done courteously and as concisely as possible. Sometimes called direct selling, this is simply giving a "sales pitch" to a prospective customer on a one-on-one basis. You will want to describe your product or service clearly and present yourself as a professional.

Sending press releases to newspapers, writing human interest articles concerning your work, or appearing on a television talk show are excellent, free ways to promote your business. Doing a fashion show, giving a lecture, or public speaking can go a long way to sitr up enthusiasm for your product or service. In all these areas, you should highlight interesting facts about your product or work that are of general interest first, and after attention is gained, you can mention your availability for business.

In conclusion, although you may be an expert in your craft, advertising and promotion could seem out of your realm. The community college in my area offered a seminar on these subjects, but the times were inconvenient for me. I bought the textbook for the course and it helped me immensely. You will also find many books that are easy to understand on advertising, promotion, and marketing at the library, and don't forget the Small Business Administration as an additional source of information. Of course, if your budget allows, you can always pay an advertising agency or publicist for these services.

By far, the very best way to get business is by word-of-mouth because you are being recommended by some one who is already satisfied with your work. Word-of-mouth is free and it will spread news of your reputation quickly, whether it is good or bad. Because of this, you should always maintain the highest standards by doing the best quality work.

SETTING UP SHOP

Licensing, Business Name, Business Types
Copyrights, Trademarks, & Patents

Before starting operations, you will need to call your local Bureau of Licenses to see if you need a license to do business in your location. They will tell you the requirements and provide you with an application. Generally anyone who is receiving money in exchange for goods or services needs a license.

As you can see from the following sample business license application, it will not be a difficult or expensive procedure. The fee will vary from city to city and usually the application must be renewed each year.

APPLICATION FOR
CITY BUSINESS LICENSE

PLEASE PRINT OR TYPE   PLEASE PRINT OR TYPE

1. To be issued to_____
                        (Name of owner, partners or corporation) (First name, middle name and last name of individuals)

2. Check one: ☐ Individual Proprietorship   ☐ Partnership   ☐ Corporation

              ☐ Professional Corporation   ☐ Sub-Chapter "S" Corporation   ☐ Other_____

3. List owner, partners or corporate officers	Title	Residence address	Phone number

4. Assumed business name used (if any) _____

5. Business Address_____
                    (Number and street)   (City, State and Zip)   (Business phone number)

   Is this a residence? Yes___ No___ List additional business locations on reverse side.

6. Name and address of property owner of above location/s _____
_____

7. Mailing address if different than Line 5_____

8. Business Description_____
   (Indicate type of goods sold & designate whether retail, wholsale, etc. or service performed
   If application is for renting or leasing of residential or commercial property please list
   locations of property on the reverse side).

9. First date of doing business in City of Portland _____

10. Are books to be kept on a calendar_____ or fiscal _____year? If fiscal, state ending date_____

11. Is this a new business venture?_____ or a previously licensed business purchased by you?_____

12. If previously licensed business, from whom purchased? _____

13. Have you ever been licensed in Portland before?_____What year?_____Address_____

Reasonable estimated license fee (to accompany application) is calculated at the rate of 2.2% of net income subject to fee.

MINIMUM FEE IS $25.00 and is subject to adjustment upon renewal.

                                          Bureau of Licenses
Make check payable to City of Portland and mail to: 1120 SW 5th AV, Rm. 1131
                                          Portland, OR 97.204

The term "license" as used in the ordinance is not to be construed to mean a permit. The Business License Fee is for revenue purposes, and is not a regulatory permit fee. The payment of a license fee and the acceptance of such fee and issuance of a license by the city does not entitle a licensee to carry on any business not in compliance with all applicable requirements of state, federal, municipal or other law.

The undersigned declares under penalty of making a false certificate that the information given in this report is true.

DATE _____ SIGNATURE_____
                                          (Owner, Partner, Corporate Officer or other duly authorized representative)

In some cities, if the location of your home is not zoned commercially, you will need to fill out a Home Occupation Permit Application before you apply for your business license. The Bureau of Licenses will tell you where to obtain it. The purpose for this is to ensure that the operation of the business will not be objectionable to neighbors. Usually, some percentage of your neighbors will be asked to sign a petition stating that they do not object to your business. Along with this, there may be certain limitations with which you must comply. These will have to do with things such as traffic, noise, dust, smoke, heat, vibration, alteration of your home, or storage that might adversly affect the residential area.

Luckily, a home sewing business is by nature so unassuming, that it wouldn't come close to violating the tranquility of a residential area. As far as getting the neighbors to consent, many of them will probably become your best clients.

Besides being a legal requirement, you may need a license for such things as advertising, hanging out a sign, and remodeling for business purposes. Quite often a license is required for wholesale buying (see the "Wholesale Buying" chapter of this book for ones that do not). Having a license will also give you credibility for financing if you need to get a loan.

If you decide to use a business name other than your own name, you can register it with the city or county clerk where you live. Inquire at the Bureau of Licenses for the procedure in your area. This is an inexpensive measure that will insure exclusivity especially if you are going to have distinctive labels in clothing or on products you produce, or if you have a unique name that you will be using in advertising or on stationery.

For tax and bookkeeping purposes, you will need to decide what type of business yours will be: a sole proprietorship, a partnership, or a corporation. In a sole proprietorship, the business owner is responsible for financing, management decisions, and liabilities or debts of the business. This is the most simple and easiest type of business to run and will probably be the most appropriate if you are the only person involved in your business. You can start out as a sole proprietorship and change to another type in the future.

A partnership is formed when two or more individuals want to combine their money, resources, and/or talents. A partnership agreement drawn up by an attorney and signed by all of the partners becomes an enforceable contract and will list each partner's responsibilities, liabilities, and the profit distribution plan.

A corporation is a separate legal entity from its owner or owners and it limits personal liability. Going through the process of incorporating is generally not practical for a home business unless you want to expand to include stockholders, or have many personal assets (property, investments, savings, etc.) to lose should you be sued for some reason.

You will probably be asked what type of business you are if you apply for a business license or loan. For more information on all three business types, consult your library, the Small Business Adminstration, attorneys, or accountants.

Copyrights, Trademarks, & Patents

A copyright protects artistic and literary expression such as books, music, plays, motion pictures, videotapes, audiotapes, and more. In other words, it protects the manner of expression of ideas, not the ideas themselves. To copyright something you must print the word "copyright", or its abbreviation, "copr.", or the copyright symbol, ©, on it along with the year of the first publication of the work and the name of the copyright owner. This serves as notice to the public that it is illegal to copy or use the item without express permission from the copyright owner.

Registration with the U.S. Copyright Office is optional, but doing so will entitle you to sue for either actual damages and profits made by the violator or for statutory damages. For information or forms you can write to: Register of Copyrights, Copyright Office, Library of Congress, Washington, D.C., 20559.

A trademark is a word, symbol, or slogan, or a combination of the above that identifies and distinguishes the goods or services of one party from those of another. A trademark gives no exclusive rights over a product or service, but is meant to indicate the source or origin of the goods to guarantee uniform quality, and to advertise the product. It assures the consumer that what they are buying is a certain brand rather than an imitation or knock-off.

The government grants patents or property rights to inventors or their heirs for original inventions. In other words, a patent is "the right to exclude others from making, using, or selling" the invention. Patents are given only to the first inventor that files regardless if identical inventions were simultaneously invented.

For more information on patents or trademarks contact: U.S. Patent and Trademark Office, Washington, D.C., 20231. The patent and trademark office is not an enforcement agency and you as an individual or business must hire an attorney to bring suit against violators. Some states also register trademarks and you can check with your Secretary of State at your state capitol about that.

TAXES

We, as Americans, have the opportunity to succeed in sewing as a home business largely because of our great free enterprise system which is based on taxes. It is an obligation as well as a privilege to pay taxes to support such a system. The Internal Revenue Service requires self-employed people to declare their income and to pay taxes on it. You will have to educate yourself concerning tax laws so you will not be guilty of paying too much or too little.

There are two kinds of tax that will concern you as a business owner: sales tax and income tax. First I will discuss sales tax. Since there are only a few states left that do not have

STATE OF WASHINGTON
DEPARTMENT OF REVENUE
EXCISE TAX DIVISION AX-02
OLYMPIA, WASHINGTON 98504

APPLICATION FOR CERTIFICATE OF REGISTRATION

INSTRUCTIONS

SHADED AREAS FOR DEPARTMENT USE ONLY

- 1 THRU 16 MUST BE COMPLETE AND A SEPARATE CHECK FOR THE $15.00 REGISTRATION FEE SUBMITTED OR THE APPLICATION WILL NOT BE ACCEPTED. DO NOT SEND CASH.
- MAIL ORIGINAL (GREEN) COPY TO ABOVE ADDRESS. RETAIN WHITE COPY AS YOUR RECORD.

U S E R E C O R D S	ACCT TYPE	REG. NO.				
	NM	SIC		OWNER	FREQ	FORM DATE
	CIG YR	MAIL/VOLUME	BLC/Fish	EXCL	JT BRANCH	

1 DATE OF FIRST TAXABLE BUSINESS ACTIVITY IN WASHINGTON UNDER THIS OWNERSHIP · MONTH · DAY · YEAR

2 NATURE OF BUSINESS: ☐ RETAIL ☐ MANUFACTURING ☐ WHOLESALE ☐ SERVICE
IF CONSTRUCTION, SPECIFY TYPE ☐ OTHER, PLEASE SPECIFY ☐ RESIDENTIAL ☐ HIGHWAY ☐ COMMERCIAL ☐ SPECULATIVE

DESCRIBE IN DETAIL PRINCIPAL PRODUCT OR SERVICE RENDERED IN WASHINGTON
☐ FULL TIME ☐ PART TIME · NO EMPLOYEES
EST. ANNUAL GROSS INCOME

CHECK & COMPLETE ONE

3

☐ **INDIVIDUAL**

OWNER'S LAST NAME	FIRST	MIDDLE INITIAL	SOCIAL SECURITY NUMBER
SPOUSE	FIRST	MIDDLE INITIAL	SOCIAL SECURITY NUMBER

OPERATED BY HUSBAND AND WIFE? ☐ YES ☐ NO

☐ **PARTNERSHIP**

FIRST PARTNER'S LAST NAME	FIRST	MIDDLE INITIAL	SPOUSE	SOCIAL SECURITY NUMBER
SECOND PARTNER'S LAST NAME	FIRST	MIDDLE INITIAL	SPOUSE	SOCIAL SECURITY NUMBER
THIRD PARTNER'S LAST NAME (ATTACH LIST FOR ADDITIONAL PARTNERS) FIRST	MIDDLE INITIAL	SPOUSE	SOCIAL SECURITY NUMBER	

☐ **CORPORATION**

FULL LEGAL NAME OF CORPORATION	FEIN (FED. EMP. ID NO.)
NAME OF ONE OFFICER	ADDRESS	TITLE

☐ **OTHER**

NAME (ASSOCIATION AND MUNICIPAL)

4 FIRM NAME · TELEPHONE-HOME/MESSAGE ( ) · TELEPHONE-BUSINESS ( )

5 BUSINESS LOCATION (STREET OR ROUTE NUMBER, CITY, STATE) · ZIP CODE · LOCAL SALES TAX CODE

6 MAILING ADDRESS (STREET OR ROUTE NUMBER, CITY, STATE) · ZIP CODE · LOCATOR CODE

7 REASON FOR FILING THIS APPLICATION ☐ STARTING NEW BUSINESS ☐ INCORPORATING EXISTING BUSINESS ☐ CHANGE IN OWNERSHIP OF EXISTING BUSINESS ☐ CHANGE IN CORP. ENTITY
NAME, FIRM NAME AND ADDRESS OF PREVIOUS OPERATOR · REGISTRATION NUMBER

8 HAVE YOU PURCHASED ANY FIXTURES OR EQUIPMENT ON WHICH YOU HAVE NOT PAID A SALES OR USE TAX? ☐ YES ☐ NO IF YES, PURCHASE PRICE $ _____ · USE TAX

9 HAVE YOU BEEN IN BUSINESS BEFORE IN WASHINGTON STATE? (SPOUSE INCLUDED) ☐ YES ☐ NO IF YES, YEAR_____
NAME, FIRM NAME AND ADDRESS · REGISTRATION NUMBER

10 IF YOU SELL CIGARETTES, OTHER THAN THROUGH A VENDING MACHINE OWNED BY ANOTHER PERSON, YOU MUST OBTAIN A LICENSE FROM THE DEPARTMENT OF LICENSING, BUSINESS LICENSE CENTER, OLYMPIA 98504. TELEPHONE 1-800-562-8203.

11 CORPORATE INFORMATION: STATE OF INCORPORATION _____ DATE OF INCORPORATION OR DOMESTICATION _____ REGISTERED AGENT _____

12 DO YOU HAVE BRANCH LOCATIONS? ☐ YES ☐ NO · IF YES, COMPLETE SECTION 1 ON BACK

13 ARE YOU AN OUT-OF-STATE FIRM? ☐ YES ☐ NO IF YES, COMPLETE SECTION 2 ON BACK · FIELD USE ONLY · NAME · DATE

14 PERSONAL REFERENCE (NAME, ADDRESS, TELEPHONE NUMBER)

15 BANK REFERENCE (BANK, BRANCH, ACCOUNT NUMBER)

16 APPLICATION SIGNATURE · TITLE · DATE · HOME ADDRESS

REGISTRATION FEE
☐ CHECK ☐ LBX ☐ TRANS
☐ CASH ☐ BLC ☐ SPLIT W _____
DATE RECEIVED · PROCESSED BY

FORM REV 44 2401 (1 83) -293-

SECTION 1 — LIST ALL BRANCH LOCATIONS WITHIN WASHINGTON

NAME OPERATED UNDER	STREET OR ROUTE NUMBER, CITY	LOCATION OF BOOKS

SECTION 2 — OUT OF STATE FIRMS (COMPLETE ITEMS 1 THRU 6)

1 ARE SALES SOLICITED IN WASHINGTON? ☐ NO. IF YES, HOW? ☐ RESIDENT EMPLOYEES ☐ LOCAL INDEPENDENT AGENTS ☐ TRAVELING REPS. ☐ OTHER_____ ARE SALES IN ☐ YOUR NAME ☐ AGENTS NAME

IF SOLICITATION BY LOCAL INDEPENDENT AGENTS (INCLUDES BROKERS AND COMMISSION AGENTS) LIST INFORMATION BELOW.

NAME	STREET OR ROUTE NUMBER, CITY

2 DO YOU MAINTAIN LOCAL STOCKS OF MERCHANDISE (INCLUDES CONSIGNED STOCKS)? ☐ NO. IF YES, LIST LOCATIONS BELOW.

3 DO YOU LEASE ARTICLES OF TANGIBLE PERSONAL PROPERTY TO OTHERS FOR USE IN THE STATE OF WASHINGTON? ☐ NO ☐ YES

4 ARE YOU A FRANCHISOR, WITH FRANCHISEE LOCATIONS WITHIN THE STATE OF WASHINGTON? ☐ NO ☐ YES

5 DO YOU RENDER SERVICE WITHIN THE STATE OF WASHINGTON TO CUSTOMERS, CLIENTS OR FRANCHISEES? ☐ NO. IF YES, DESCRIBE BELOW.

6 LOCATION OF HOME OFFICE (STREET, CITY, STATE):

INFORMATION MAY BE OBTAINED AT THE FOLLOWING DISTRICT OFFICES:

CONSULT YOUR TELEPHONE DIRECTORY FOR TELEPHONE NUMBERS AND ADDRESS UNDER: **WASHINGTON STATE OF**

ABERDEEN	EVERETT	OLYMPIA	SEATTLE	VANCOUVER
BELLINGHAM	MOUNT VERNON	PASCO	SPOKANE	WALLA WALLA
BREMERTON	KELSO	PORT ANGELES	TACOMA	WENATCHEE
		RENTON		YAKIMA

a sales tax, collecting it will be a necessity for most businesses unless your state does not charge tax on services, clothing, or other items that you may be selling. To find out if you need to collect and pay tax and to apply for a Sales Tax Number, call or write your State Department of Taxation and Finance or your State Department of Revenue.

The application forms will be slightly different from state to state, but they are not involved or costly. I have included an application blank from the State of Washington for you to see. Some new business owners are afraid to apply for a tax number just because it includes the word "tax." In reality, this simply allows you to legally collect sales tax from your customers and to forward it to the government. Having a tax number will give your business legitimacy and enable you to buy wholesale in more places. It also prevents you from paying sales tax on goods or materials that you are going to resell.

Now I will turn to the subject of income tax. Don't be overwhelmed at the prospect of preparing your own taxes. There is much good, free, or inexpensive help available.

Check with a community college or the Small Business Administration in your area to see if they offer a Small Business Tax Seminar. This is usually a one-day class where experts in small business from the Internal Revenue Service will help interpret the laws and the forms that apply to your situation. It will be very reasonably priced and the information is invaluable.

If such a seminar is not available, call the Internal Revenue Service to order the free booklet, *Tax Guide for Small Businesses*. The Internal Revenue Service is listed under the "Department of the Treasury" in the phone book. Set aside some time to study this information-packed publication. It will take the mystery out of your tax preparation by discussing every aspect of taxation. It will also list all the forms and publications that you will need to figure your taxes.

Each I.R.S. form has its own booklet to aid you in filling it out and it becomes a matter of putting the right information into the right blanks. Since you are the one who will be recording all receipts and expenditures, it is possible if not advisable for you to do your own taxes.

Most self-employed people need to fill out the form 1040-ES which is titled, "Estimated Tax for Individuals." You will need to begin estimating your tax payments and you will be responsible for paying quarterly or four times a year. After you fill it out the first time, you will be sent vouchers for making the remaining payments. Instead of having an employer take taxes out of your paychecks, you will be responsible for making the payments yourself. At the end of the year you will file a regular 1040 like everyone else and you may need to pay more tax or you may be due a refund.

Self-employed people also fill out Schedule SE, "Computation of Social Security Self-Employment Tax." I have pictured this form on the following pages. Again, where previously an employer would have figured and deducted your Social Security Tax, you will now do it yourself. When you figure the amount and transfer it to your 1040 form, it will automatically be credited to your Social Security account when you file the return. Other forms you need could include, "Profit and Loss from a Business," "Depreciation and Amortization," "Interest Income," and "Itemized Deductions."

Self-Employment Tax

▶ **See Instructions for Schedule SE (Form 1040).**

▶ **Attach to Form 1040.**

OMB No. 1545-0074

Attachment
Sequence No. **17**

Name of person with **self-employment** income (as shown on Form 1040) | Social security number of person with **self-employment** income ▶

Who Must File Schedule SE

You must file Schedule SE if:

- Your wages (and tips) subject to social security AND Medicare tax (or railroad retirement tax) were less than $135,000; **AND**
- Your net earnings from self-employment from other than church employee income (line 4 of Short Schedule SE or line 4c of Long Schedule SE) were $400 or more; **OR**
- You had church employee income of $108.28 or more. Income from services you performed as a minister or a member of a religious order is **not** church employee income. See page SE-1.

Note: *Even if you have a loss or a small amount of income from self-employment, it may be to your benefit to file Schedule SE and use either "optional method" in Part II of Long Schedule SE. See page SE-3.*

Exception. If your only self-employment income was from earnings as a minister, member of a religious order, or Christian Science practitioner, **AND** you filed Form 4361 and received IRS approval not to be taxed on those earnings, **DO NOT** file Schedule SE. Instead, write "Exempt–Form 4361" on Form 1040, line 47.

May I Use Short Schedule SE or MUST I Use Long Schedule SE?

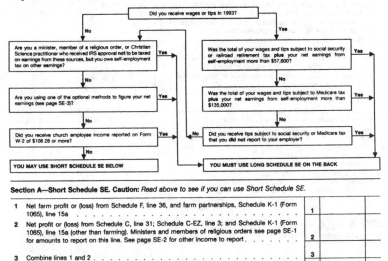

Section A—Short Schedule SE. Caution: *Read above to see if you can use Short Schedule SE.*

1	Net farm profit or (loss) from Schedule F, line 36, and farm partnerships, Schedule K-1 (Form 1065), line 15a	**1**	
2	Net profit or (loss) from Schedule C, line 31; Schedule C-EZ, line 3; and Schedule K-1 (Form 1065), line 15a (other than farming). Ministers and members of religious orders see page SE-1 for amounts to report on this line. See page SE-2 for other income to report	**2**	
3	Combine lines 1 and 2	**3**	
4	**Net earnings from self-employment.** Multiply line 3 by 92.35% (.9235). If less than $400, do not file this schedule; you do not owe self-employment tax . . . . ▶	**4**	
5	Self-employment tax. If the amount on line 4 is: • $57,600 or less, multiply line 4 by 15.3% (.153) and enter the result. • More than $57,600 but less than $135,000, multiply the amount in excess of $57,600 by 2.9% (.029). Then, add $8,812.80 to the result and enter the total. • $135,000 or more, enter $11,057.40. Also enter on Form 1040, **line 47. (Important:** You are allowed a deduction for one-half of this amount. Multiply line 5 by 50% (.5) and enter the result on **Form 1040, line 25.)**	**5**	

For Paperwork Reduction Act Notice, see Form 1040 Instructions. | Cat. No. 11358Z | **Schedule SE (Form 1040)**

Name of person with **self-employment** income (as shown on Form 1040)	Social security number of person with **self-employment** income ▶

Section B—Long Schedule SE

Part I   Self-Employment Tax

Note: If your only income subject to self-employment tax is church employee income, skip lines 1 through 4b. Enter -0- on line 4c and go to line 5a. Income from services you performed as a minister or a member of a religious order is not church employee income. See page SE-1.

A   If you are a minister, member of a religious order, or Christian Science practitioner AND you filed Form 4361, but you had $400 or more of **other** net earnings from self-employment, check here and continue with Part I . . . . . . ▶ ☐

1	Net farm profit or (loss) from Schedule F, line 36, and farm partnerships, Schedule K-1 (Form 1065), line 15a. **Note:** Skip this line if you use the farm optional method. See page SE-3 . .	1	
2	Net profit or (loss) from Schedule C, line 31; Schedule C-EZ, line 3; and Schedule K-1 (Form 1065), line 15a (other than farming). Ministers and members of religious orders see page SE-1 for amounts to report on this line. See page SE-2 for other income to report. **Note:** Skip this line if you use the nonfarm optional method. See page SE-3	2	
3	Combine lines 1 and 2	3	
4a	If line 3 is more than zero, multiply line 3 by 92.35% (.9235). Otherwise, enter amount from line 3	4a	
b	If you elected one or both of the optional methods, enter the total of lines 17 and 19 here . .	4b	
c	Combine lines 4a and 4b. If less than $400, **do not** file this schedule; you do not owe self-employment tax. **Exception.** If less than $400 and you had church employee income, enter -0- and continue . ▶	4c	
5a	Enter your church employee income from Form W-2. **Caution:** See page SE-1 for definition of church employee income 5a		
b	Multiply line 5a by 92.35% (.9235). If less than $100, enter -0-	5b	
6	**Net earnings from self-employment.** Add lines 4c and 5b	6	
7	Maximum amount of combined wages and self-employment earnings subject to social security tax or the 6.2% portion of the 7.65% railroad retirement (tier 1) tax for 1993	7	
8a	Total social security wages and tips (from Form(s) W-2) and railroad retirement (tier 1) compensation 8a		
b	Unreported tips subject to social security tax (from Form 4137, line 9) 8b		
c	Add lines 8a and 8b	8c	
9	Subtract line 8c from line 7. If zero or less, enter -0- here and on line 10 and go to line 12a ▶	9	
10	Multiply the **smaller** of line 6 or line 9 by 12.4% (.124)	10	
11	Maximum amount of combined wages and self-employment earnings subject to Medicare tax or the 1.45% portion of the 7.65% railroad retirement (tier 1) tax for 1993	11	
12a	Total Medicare wages and tips (from Form(s) W-2) and railroad retirement (tier 1) compensation 12a		
b	Unreported tips subject to Medicare tax (from Form 4137, line 14) . 12b		
c	Add lines 12a and 12b	12c	
13	Subtract line 12c from line 11. If zero or less, enter -0- here and on line 14 and go to line 15 .	13	
14	Multiply the **smaller** of line 6 or line 13 by 2.9% (.029)	14	
15	**Self-employment tax.** Add lines 10 and 14. Enter here and on **Form 1040, line 47.** (Important: You are allowed a deduction for **one-half** of this amount. Multiply line 15 by 50% (.5) and enter the result on **Form 1040, line 25.)**	15	

Part II   Optional Methods To Figure Net Earnings (See page SE-3.)

Farm Optional Method. You may use this method only if **(a)** Your gross farm income[1] was not more than $2,400 or **(b)** Your gross farm income[1] was more than $2,400 and your net farm profits[2] were less than $1,733.

16	Maximum income for optional methods	16	
17	Enter the **smaller** of: two-thirds (⅔) of gross farm income[1] (not less than zero) **or** $1,600. Also, include this amount on line 4b above	17	

Nonfarm Optional Method. You may use this method only if **(a)** Your net nonfarm profits[3] were less than $1,733 and also less than 72.189% of your gross nonfarm income,[4] **and (b)** You had net earnings from self-employment of at least $400 in 2 of the prior 3 years. **Caution:** You may use this method no more than five times.

18	Subtract line 17 from line 16	18	
19	Enter the **smaller** of: two-thirds (⅔) of gross nonfarm income[4] (not less than zero) or the amount on line 18. Also, include this amount on line 4b above	19	

[1]From Schedule F, line 11, and Schedule K-1 (Form 1065), line 15b.   [3]From Schedule C, line 31; Schedule C-EZ, line 3; and Schedule K-1 (Form 1065), line 15a.
[2]From Schedule F, line 36, and Schedule K-1 (Form 1065), line 15a.   [4]From Schedule C, line 7; Schedule C-EZ, line 1; and Schedule K-1 (Form 1065), line 15c.

SCHEDULE C-EZ
(Form 1040)

Department of the Treasury
Internal Revenue Service   (10)

Net Profit From Business
(Sole Proprietorship)

▶ Partnerships, joint ventures, etc., must file Form 1065.

▶ **Attach to Form 1040 or Form 1041.** ▶ **See Instructions on back.**

OMB No. 1545-0074

Attachment
Sequence No. **09A**

Name of proprietor | Social security number (SSN)

Part I   General Information

You May Use This Schedule Only If You:

- Had gross receipts from your business of $25,000 or less.
- Had business expenses of $2,000 or less.
- Use the cash method of accounting.
- Did not have an inventory at any time during the year.
- Did not have a net loss from your business.
- Had only one business as a sole proprietor.

And You:

- Had no employees during the year.
- Are not required to file Form 4562, Depreciation and Amortization, for this business. See the instructions for Schedule C, line 13, on page C-3 to find out if you must file.
- Do not deduct expenses for business use of your home.
- Do not have prior year unallowed passive activity losses from this business.

A Principal business or profession, including product or service

B Enter principal business code (see page C-6) ▶

C Business name. If no separate business name, leave blank.

D Employer ID number (EIN), if any

E Business address (including suite or room no.). Address not required if same as on Form 1040, page 1.

City, town or post office, state, and ZIP code

Part II   Figure Your Net Profit

1 **Gross receipts.** If more than $25,000, you **must** use Schedule C.
Caution: *If this income was reported to you on Form W-2 and the "Statutory employee" box on that form was checked, see Statutory Employees in the instructions for Schedule C, line 1, on page C-2 and check here* . . . . ▶ ☐   **1**

2 **Total expenses.** If more than $2,000, you **must** use Schedule C. See instructions **2**

3 **Net profit.** Subtract line 2 from line 1. If less than zero, you **must** use Schedule C. Enter on **Form 1040, line 12,** and ALSO on **Schedule SE, line 2.** (Statutory employees **do not** report this amount on Schedule SE, line 2. Estates and trusts, enter on Form 1041, line 3.) **3**

Part III   Information on Your Vehicle. Complete this part ONLY if you are claiming car or truck expenses on line 2.

4 When did you place your vehicle in service for business purposes? (month, day, year) ▶ ..... / ..... / ..... .

5 Of the total number of miles you drove your vehicle during 1994, enter the number of miles you used your vehicle for:

a Business .... **b** Commuting .... **c** Other ....

6 Do you (or your spouse) have another vehicle available for personal use? . . . . ☐ **Yes** ☐ **No**

7 Was your vehicle available for use during off-duty hours? . . . . ☐ **Yes** ☐ **No**

8a Do you have evidence to support your deduction? . . . . ☐ **Yes** ☐ **No**

b If "Yes," is the evidence written? . . . . ☐ **Yes** ☐ **No**

For Paperwork Reduction Act Notice, see Form 1040 Instructions.   Cat. No. 14374D   Schedule C-EZ (Form 1040)

It is a common misconception among business owners to think that they can go to a tax consultant and miraculously save hundreds of dollars on their taxes. This may happen, but only if the consultant is as familiar with the workings of your business as you are, and this can only be accomplished by you paying for hours of time to familiarize the consultant with your business. If you don't trust yourself or just can't stand the thought of doing your own taxes, you will save time and money by presenting orderly and legible records to a tax consultant.

Lastly, people who make mistakes in figuring their taxes do not go to jail. It is the people who do not claim income that the Internal Revenue Service finds fault with. This does not mean you won't get audited if you claim all of your income and figure your taxes. The I.R.S. may disagree with, misunderstand, or find a mistake in some calculation you have made. If you have made a diligent effort to figure your taxes and can document your transactions, you will always receive a chance to correct errors or to prove your original claim.

INSURANCE and RETIREMENT

Insurance coverage has traditionally been one of the great benefits that is included as part of your compensation when working for someone else, but this will be your own responsibility as a self-employed person. There are different types of insurance that cover different needs so you will need to assess which are right for you.

Liability insurance pays for bodily injury to customers while they are on your property. If a customer would fall down your steps or slip on a wet floor while in your home, you could be considered liable. This may be covered under your homeowners policy, but if not, special policies or riders are available.

Personal property insurance covers damage to your property (machines, fabric, furniture, etc.) and to your customer's garments caused by fire, water, or theft. If you own a home, sometimes your homeowner's insurance will cover this, but don't take a chance and assume that it will. If you live in an apartment, you may want to investigate the purchase of a renter's policy, but again, check for the business coverage.

You may also want to investigate disability insurance since a disability to you could result in the immediate cessation of your business. Key man insurance is a type of disability insurance which continues to pay a salary to the key person in a business if that person becomes disabled and is unable to work for a period of time.

Life insurance is one of the most well-known types of insurance and there are many, many types of policies available. In general, if you are a single person without children, life insurance is usually not a necessity.

Because the number of self-employed people is growing rapidly in our country, options for health insurance are gowing too. If you are not married or cannot get coverage under a spouse's plan, call different insurance companies to see if they offer plans you might use. The National Association for the Self-Employed offers policies for individuals. You can call 800-232-6273 to find out about the association and their insurance plans.

The Small Business Adminstration has given out some excellent guidelines to help you study and compare insurance costs. They are as follows:

1. Decide what perils to insure against and how much loss you might suffer from each.

2. Cover your largest loss exposure first.

3. Use as high a deductible as you can afford.

4. Avoid duplication in insurance.

5. Buy in as large a unit as possible. Many of the "package policies" are very suitable for the types of small businesses they are designed to serve, and often they are the only way a small business can get really adequate protection.

6. Review your insurance program periodically to make sure that your coverage is adequate and your premiums are as low as possible.

Along with insurance coverage, self-employed people are also responsible for their own retirement plans. According to the Social Security Adminstration, middle income retirees will need to provide more than half of their income from their own savings or investments in the future.

An IRA is still one of the best methods of "do it yourself" retirement planning. In addition to having a built-in growth plan and higher interest rates than a savings account, IRA contributions may be tax deductible. You deposit money in an IRA (up to $2,000 per year) each year until April 15, and you cannot withdraw it until you become a certain age without a penalty.

Keoghs are another similar way to build a retirement account for people who want to consistently deposit more than $2,000 per year in an investment plan. With Keoghs, you must deposit the money by December 31 each year. You can contact your bank or any investment firm for more information on these.

FINANCING YOUR BUSINESS

One of the major advantages of operating a sewing business in your home is that in general, you will have very few if any start-up costs. In most cases, you can simply use your sewing area and the equipment you already have. If, however, you decide you need to expand or purchase new equipment or supplies, you may need financing.

If you are applying for a loan from a bank, credit union, or other financial institution, you will probably need to fill out a financial statement. There are individual financial statements and business financial statements. I have included a typical form for an individual financial statement. You would not fill out a business financial statement, which is much longer and more detailed, until your business has shown a profit for more than several years.

FINANCIAL STATEMENT

Personal Form

(DO NOT USE FOR BUSINESS)

The undersigned, for the purpose of inducing you to provide the undersigned with merchant services, furnishes the following as being a true and correct statement of the financial condition of the undersigned as of the above date, and agrees to notify you immediately of any material change in said financial condition. The undersigned agrees that you may immediately terminate the merchant services without notice if (i) the undersigned breaches any agreement with you, (ii) any of the information provided below proves to be untrue or the undersigned fails to notify you of any material change as above agreed, (iii) the undersigned deposits unlawful transactions in the undersigned's account, (iv) the undersigned's account has been inactive for six (6) months, (v) the undersigned changes productline or the location from which the undersigned conducts business, (vi) the undersigned becomes insolvent or subject to bankruptcy proceedings, or (vii) anything happens that causes you to believe in good faith that the undersigned may be unable or unwilling to meet the undersigned's obligations under the Merchant Agreement.

TO: **First Interstate Bank**		OFFICE			NO.	SOCIAL SECURITY NO.
NAME	ADDRESS	CITY	STATE	ZIP CODE		HOME TELEPHONE NO.
EMPLOYER NAME & ADDRESS		POSITION HELD				BUSINESS PHONE
SPOUSE-CO-APPLICANT NAME	SOC. SEC. NO.	FINANCIAL CONDITION AS OF				, 19

ASSETS				LIABILITIES		
CASH IN THIS BANK	(Checking) DEMAND			NOTES PAYABLE TO THIS BANK (Sch 4)		
	(Savings) TIME			NOTES PAYABLE TO OTHER BANKS AND OTHER FINANCIAL INSTITUTIONS (Sch 4)		
CASH IN OTHER FINANCIAL INSTITUTIONS	(Checking) DEMAND			CURRENT BILLS PAYABLE (Other than Installment Loans)		
	(Savings) TIME					
ACCOUNTS RECEIVABLE				INCOME AND OTHER TAXES PAYABLE		
NOTES OR MORTGAGES RECEIVABLE (Due within one year) (Sch 1)				DUE TO BROKERS		
STOCKS AND BONDS — LISTED ON MAJOR EXCHANGES (Sch 2)						

CURRENT ASSETS			CURRENT LIABILITIES		
REAL ESTATE AND BUILDINGS (Sch. 3)			LOANS ON LIFE INSURANCE (Sch. 5)		
AUTOMOBILE AND OTHER VEHICLES — MARKET VALUE (Describe)			OTHER LONG TERM OBLIGATIONS (Due after one year) (Sch. 4)		
HOUSEHOLD GOODS AND OTHER PERSONAL PROPERTY (Describe)					
OTHER SECURITIES (Sch. 2)					
CASH VALUE LIFE INSURANCE (Sch. 5)					
LONG TERM RECEIVABLES (Due after one year) (Sch. 1)					
OTHER					
			TOTAL LIABILITIES		
			NET WORTH		
TOTAL ASSETS			TOTAL LIABILITIES AND NET WORTH		

GROSS INCOME	Monthly	Annual	FIXED EXPENSE	Monthly	Annual
Alimony, child support, or separate maintenance income need not be revealed if you do not wish to have it considered as a basis for repaying this obligation					
SALARY			INSURANCE PREMIUMS		
SPOUSE'S SALARY			RENTAL		
INCOME FROM SECURITIES (Sch. 2)			R.E. MTGE. & INSTALMENT PAYMENTS (Sch. 4)		
RENTAL OR LEASE INCOME (Sch. 3)			INCOME AND OTHER TAXES		
MORTGAGES OR CONTRACT INCOME (Sch. 3)			OTHER		
OTHER					
TOTAL GROSS INCOME			TOTAL FIXED EXPENSE		

SCHEDULE 1. NOTES, CONTRACTS, AND MORTGAGES RECEIVABLE

DUE FROM	AMOUNT DUE		DATE OF MATURITY	AMT. OF PAYMENT REC'D.		TYPE OF OBLIGATION AND COLLATERAL IF SECURED
	WITHIN ONE YEAR	AFTER ONE YEAR		MONTHLY	ANNUALLY	
TOTALS						

SCHEDULE 2. STOCKS AND BONDS (ATTACH SEPARATE SHEET IF NECESSARY)

No. of Shares or Face Value Bonds	DESCRIPTION	SECURITY IN NAME OF	MARKET PRICE	Current Market Value		Bond Information	Annual Income on Securities
				LISTED	UNLISTED	INTEREST RATE AND MATURITY DATE	
			TOTALS				

ARE ANY OF THESE SECURITIES PLEDGED TO SECURE BROKERS LOANS? IF SO, GIVE DETAILS, _____

SCHEDULE 3. REAL ESTATE AND BUILDINGS

YEAR PURCH.	LOCATION AND DESCRIPTION	TITLE IN NAME OF	COST			MARKET VALUE	DEBT (SEE SCH. 4)	INCOME
			LAND	IMP	TOTAL			
		TOTALS						

AMOUNT OF FIRE INSURANCE FOR EACH LOCATION _____
ARE ANY TAXES DELINQUENT? _____ IF SO, GIVE AMOUNT AND DETAILS _____
HAVE YOU FILED A HOMESTEAD? _____ IF SO, GIVE LOCATION _____

SCHEDULE 4. NOTES, CONTRACTS, AND MORTGAGES PAYABLE (INCLUDE REAL ESTATE MORTGAGES)

DUE TO	AMOUNT DUE		DATE OF MATURITY	AMOUNT OF PAYMENT		TYPE OF OBLIGATION AND COLLATERAL IF SECURED
	WITHIN ONE YEAR	AFTER ONE YEAR		MONTHLY	ANNUALLY	
TOTALS						

IF ANY PAYMENTS OF PRINCIPAL OR INTEREST ARE DELINQUENT, PLEASE GIVE DETAILS _____

SCHEDULE 5. LIFE INSURANCE

NAME OF COMPANY	BENEFICIARY	FACE AMOUNT	CASH VALUE	AMOUNT OF LOAN	DUE TO
		TOTALS			

AUTO INSURANCE
PUBLIC LIABILITY $ _____ PROPERTY DAMAGE $ _____ HEALTH, ACCIDENT, DISABILITY YES _____ NO _____
HAVE YOU ANY LIABILITY AS GUARANTOR OR ENDORSER? YES _____ NO _____ IF SO, GIVE DETAILS _____

HAVE YOU EVER DECLARED BANKRUPTCY? YES _____ NO _____ IF SO, GIVE DATE _____
ARE YOU MARRIED? YES _____ NO _____ IF SO, ARE THE ABOVE ASSETS YOUR SPOUSE'S _____ SEPARATE _____
PROPERTY? DESCRIBE _____
ARE THERE ANY SUITS, JUDGMENTS, TAX DEFICIENCIES OR OTHER CLAIMS PENDING OR IN PROCESS AGAINST YOU? YES _____ NO _____
GIVE DETAILS _____
HAVE YOU MADE A WILL? YES _____ NO _____ IF SO, WHO IS NAMED EXECUTOR OF ESTATE? _____

THIS STATEMENT HAS BEEN REVIEWED BY THE UNDERSIGNED OFFICER OF THIS BANK.	In submitting the foregoing statement, both the printed and written portions of which I have carefully read, I guarantee its accuracy with the intent it be relied upon by you in providing merchant services to me. I warrant that I have no known obligations, direct or contingent, which have not been set forth hereon and that I have not knowingly withheld any material information of an adverse nature. I hereby authorize you to investigate my credit record and to check statements I've made

DATE	BANK OFFICER	DATE SIGNED	SIGNATURE
		DATE SIGNED	SIGNATURE (CO-APPLICANT)

You will fill in the blanks with information concerning your income, expenditures, assets, and liabilities. If you do not understand some of the categories, always ask for interpretation. When you have completed your financial statement, you will submit it with your loan application.

When reviewing a loan application, the lending institution will look first and foremost at the character of the applicant. When a bank is the lender, knowing your banker and having an established history with the bank will be your biggest asset. The following are some questions to consider:

Do you present yourself as a professional?

Do you have or are you opening a business account?

Are you organized and prepared?

Are you on time?

Do you have the skills to accomplish your goals?

What are your past achievements?

Include a business card and a brochure or promotional literature about yourself if you have any. Anything that sheds light on you or your business will help.

Next, the lender will want to know what you are going to do with the money. How will your business improve because of it? Are you going to purchase equipment? If so, what, and have you shopped for prices? How much more will you be able to produce with the use of it? How will you repay the loan and under what time frame? Write down the answers to all these questions in a logical order and include any other pertinent information that might prove your case. Present it to the institution along with your financial statement and the loan application.

Your entire package will be reviewed within a few days or it could take as long as several weeks. If you do not have the collateral or the income to show that you can repay the loan, it will be your job to convince the lender that you have other means to do so. Your ability as a business person, your projected sales, previous tax returns, and proof of your past business or management successes are all things that could help.

When an application for a loan has been rejected, the institution will tell you the specific reason. Sometimes it is a matter of not supplying enough information or of not putting information in the right blank. Communication is the key here. Go over the application carefully and question the loan officer. Maybe you can do more research or supply more data.

If, after all this, you are still rejected, you will have a few alternatives. The Small Business Administration helps small businesses obtain loans from other institutions and guarantees them. Call the Small Business Administration in your area for more information on this and related services.

As an alternative, many small business owners find it quicker and easier to use credit cards instead of applying for a loan. If this is an option for you, be sure to know the interest rates, both for purchases and for cash advances as they are usually different. Make a plan to pay off your charges just as you would a loan. (If you want to have customers pay you with credit cards, see the chapter on "Pricing".)

As time goes on, you will have been in business longer and you will be making more money. Your financial situation will change and you will become a better credit risk.

BOOKKEEPING

Bookkeeping can be a dreaded word for self-employed people, especially for creative entrepreneurs. We want to spend our time doing our craft, not keeping books. Because you are probably working by yourself in your home, you will be amazed to learn how simple your bookkeeping can be. I highly recommend that you set up a system of bookkeeping before you start your business. You will not end up procrastinating this part of your business if you keep records as you go. If you are already in business without a system, set aside some time to implement one.

I am going to explain the basics of bookkeeping and try to simplify the process for you. I highly recommend the Small Business Adminstration, community colleges, and bookkeeping texts as additional resources.

The two basic systems or methods of bookkeeping are cash and accrual. You will probably use the cash system which is commonly known as cash-and-carry. With the accrual system you have accounts receivable which means you allow customers to pay after you bill them. You can see how it would be more complicated because it involves bill collecting. You may start out using one system and switch to the other, but the I.R.S. will find fault if you try to alternate the two.

After you have chosen your method, the second step is to open a checking account for your business that will be separate from your personal account. This checking account will help serve as a record of deposits and expenditures and it will give you credibility as an established business in the eyes of loan officers and wholesalers. It will also give you the benefit of great personal satisfaction since your transactions will not be blending into your personal or family account.

Income will be the most pleasant data you have to record. You can do this easily by keeping a receipt pad for all your orders. These are available at any office supply store and come in duplicate or triplicate. One copy should go to the customer and at least one copy should be kept for your records. Weekly, monthly, or yearly, you will use these figures from the receipt pad to document income. I have pictured a basic sample receipt on the next page.

Now you'll need to keep a record of expenditures. Your cancelled checks will help here, but if you have paid for goods with cash or credit card, you will need a receipt. Every time you spend money for business purposes, get a receipt. Following are some examples of expenses you'll need receipts for: fabric, notions, machines and repairs of them, office supplies, copies, postage, gas used for business, licenses, attorney's fees, business cards, and any other item or service. I suggest you get twelve envelopes, one for each month. Put the receipts into the envelope and at the end of the month you can record all of them in a simple notebook or in a fancy ledger designed for that purpose.

MARY A. ROEHR
Custom Tailoring
500 Saddlerock Circle
Sedona, AZ 86336
520-282-4971

Customer's
Phone no. _____ **Date** _____

Name _____

Address _____

SOLD BY	CASH	C. O. D.	CHARGE	ON ACCT.	MDSE. RETD.	PAID OUT	

QUAN.	DESCRIPTION	PRICE	AMOUNT

I also keep track of all my monthly bills for rent/mortgage, utilities, phone, garbage, insurance, property taxes, etc., in the same way. This helps when figuring overhead expenses and is also necessary if you are going to claim part of your home for business use on your income tax return.

For the accrual system, you still need a record of all expenditures and receipts. In this case you will have "accounts receivable" which means people owe you money and you will have to give or send them a bill or invoice. If you can't afford specially printed invoices in the beginning, purchase a blank pad at an office supply store and affix your business name with a rubber stamp in order to look more professional.

When you have chosen a bookkeeping system, purchased whatever business forms you need, and provided a ledger or notebook in which to record all transactions, you have "set up your books." From them you will draw the figures to fill in all the blanks on the tax forms. You will also use the data to fill out loan and credit applications and to complete a profit and loss statement if you ever need one.

You can hire a professional to do this, but you will still have to prepare an accurate and detailed list of all your business transactions to present to an accountant. But remember, no one will have as strong an interest in your business as you do, and by keeping your own books, you will know exactly where the business stands and where it should be headed. As time goes on, you will become more sophisticated in your bookkeeping because you will understand the reason for it.

WORK ENVIRONMENT and EQUIPMENT

Your work environment and equipment will consist basically of two areas, your sewing area and your sales or fitting area. These may be combined into one space or they may be separated. The size of the areas and degree of decoration will depend on your resources and your personal style.

For the purpose of discussion, let us assume that your sales and fitting area will be separate from your sewing area. You will use the sales and fitting area to meet customers, to discuss future work, to do fittings, and to deliver completed garments or products. Since a first impression is so important, this area should be neat, attractive, and bright.

If you are doing any type of custom sewing or alterations, you will need a changing area which allows privacy for the customer. This can be as elaborate as a special enclosed room, or as simple as a drawn curtain or screen. If a bathroom is nearby, it could also be used for this purpose.

A full length mirror with good lighting is essential as is a place to sit and to put pins, chalk, sales book, business cards, tape measure, and yardstick. A clock, a calendar, and a phone will be helpful for you and your customers.

This room is a good place to display your license and other credentials such as diplomas, certificates of achievement, or awards you have won in your profession. You may also want to hang a bulletin board to show pictures of completed work, fashion illustrations, or other interesting visuals. It is a good idea to make it perfectly clear from the beginning whether the area is smoking or non-smoking. You can do this verbally or with a small sign placed in a prominent position.

Your sewing area should be as comfortable and convenient as possible. This will be your private domain and how you feel in it will affect the work you do. Of course, the ultimate is to have your own separate room, but don't be discouraged if you have only a small corner or part of a room. My current sewing room is 15' x 20', but the most efficient sewing room I ever had was in an old linen closet that measured 6' x 12'. The smaller the space you put your equipment into, the more efficient you will be because you are taking fewer steps between each piece. The advantage of a larger room is for extra storage, shelving, and cutting and pressing areas.

Good lighting is of utmost importance for sewing and a combination of natural and artificial light is desirable. Poor lighting contributes substantially to eye strain, so install a high-intensity lamp or drafting lamp if you need extra light for detail work. Take advantage of natural light whenever possible by surrounding yourself with colors that will reflect light.

A comfortable chair is essential. Take turns using all the different chairs in your home to help decide which is best. If none work, go to an office furniture store and sit in every available chair. This will probably be the most important piece of furniture in your sewing room.

I made an inexpensive cutting and pressing table from a door that I bought at the building supply store. Since it is padded and covered, I didn't need top quality or solid wood. I padded it with wool (an army blanket works well) and covered it with cotton drill, a heavy canvas-like fabric. For stability and extra storage, I placed it on filing cabinets bolstered with blocks of wood to a comfortable height. If you don't have enough room for a whole door, use as big a piece of plywood or pressed wood as your area will allow.

Other conveniences are a mirror, hanging space, bulletin board, and bookshelf. Labeled storage bins or drawers for notions and findings are handy for keeping these small articles organized. Sometimes a mannequin is helpful for fitting or for draping a garment in progress. A portable storage box is handy for carrying work from one room to another if you must do different jobs in different places.

There are several companies that supply sewing room furniture as well as articles and books on sewing room designs. Check with your sewing machine dealer, fabric store, and library for available sources.

The bare essentials of equipment for most home sewing businesses are a home sewing machine, shears, and an iron. All of these can be upgraded or changed as your business expands and as your expertise increases. Whether you replace your home machine with an industrial, or purchase an industrial in addition will be determined by your personal preference and the type of work you are doing. Some sewers find industrial machines too fast for detail work and others prefer the speed. Industrial machines will be much sturdier, and hence, much heavier than home machines. They will sew much faster but may do only one or a limited number of stitches.

The warranties on some home sewing machines are void if the machine is used for business, so this may be a consideration. Use common sense and sew on both home and industrial machines to determine which best fits your needs. Several of the sources in the chapter on "Wholesale Buying" offer industrial machines.

Types and models of sergers are now as plentiful as regular sewing machines. If you do not own a serger but want to purchase one, you should first decide exactly what you want to use it for, such as overcasting seams, actually sewing garments together, embellishment, home dec, etc., then shop from the standpoint of filling your needs rather than by trying to compare all the bells and whistles of each brand.

Juki Lock home sergers (one is pictured below) are easy to use, and are known for their high quality and performance.

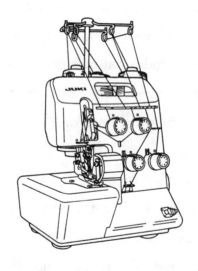

Whether you are new to serging or not, I highly recommend *Serger Update*, a monthly newsletter all about serging put out by PJS Publications, the same publisher of *Sew News*. Call 800-521-2885 for subscription information.

Viking Sewing Machine Company has long been known for quality sewing machines and sergers. From their many different models, I have pictured the Viking Husqvarna #1+ machine and the Viking Huskylock™ 1001L (Viking and Husqvarna are registered trademarks). To locate the dealer nearest you call 800-358-0001.

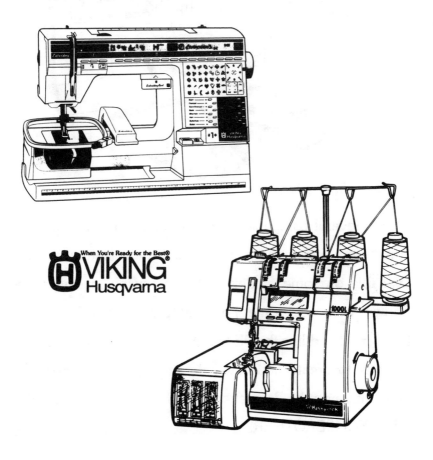

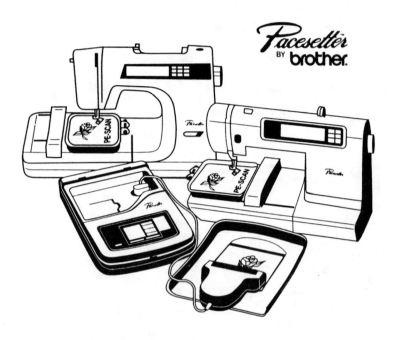

Several companies offer machines that specifically do embroidery and monogramming, but these features are now available on some models of home sewing machines also. Shown here are some Personal Embroidery Systems by Brother. By adding the PE-SCAN, you can even draw or trace pictures to create your own designer patterns. For more information on the Pacesetter and other machines by Brother, call 1-800-42BROTHER.

Singer, one of the oldest names in sewing machines, now has the Quintessence™ Quantum XL-100, a sewing machine with an embroidery bed which is shown below. Also featured is Singer's serger model 14U595. Call 908-225-8844 for more information or a dealer near you.

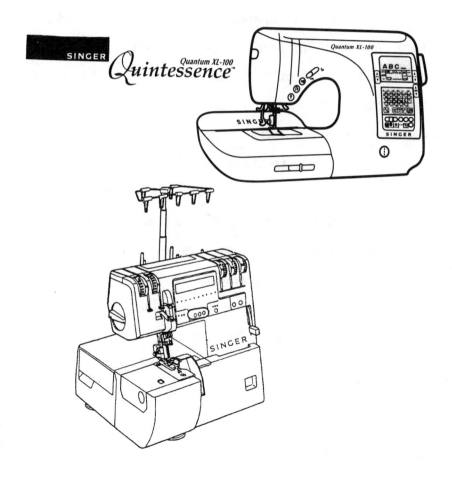

One specialty machine that you may consider purchasing is a hemming machine. Hemming machines use a single thread (no bobbin) and can be adjusted according to the weight of the fabric to make a blind hem that doesn't show on the right side of the fabric. They work very quickly and can do a hem in seconds compared to the tedium of a hand-sewn hem. Industrial and home models are both available. If you purchase one, I recommend using regular thread in a color that matches the garment instead of plastic thread which can come out or snag on socks or pantyhose. Changing thread to match the fabric is fast and easy and the results are worth it. A hemming machine can pay for itself quickly, especially if you are doing alterations or draperies, and remember that any equipment you purchase for your business is tax deductible.

Baby Lock, the company that produced the first sergers on the homesewing market, now manufactures a hemming machine which I have pictured on the opposite page. It is called the Blindhemmer and its features include dial adjustable stitch depth and length to customize the stitch to every fabric. It also uses conventional needles for easy replacement. For more information call 800-422-2952.

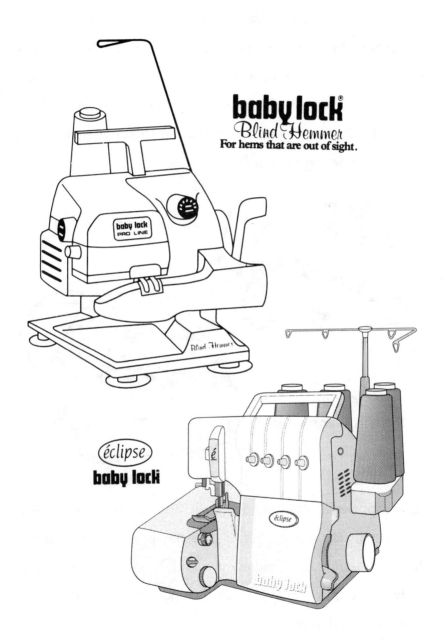

baby lock®
Blind Hemmer
For hems that are out of sight.

Features to look for in a good iron are as much weight as possible to help you with pressing, a shot of steam and/or spray for extra moisture when needed, and even distribution of steam vents on the bottom of the iron. Rowenta has long been a leading name in irons and two are featured here. Look for them in department or fabric stores.

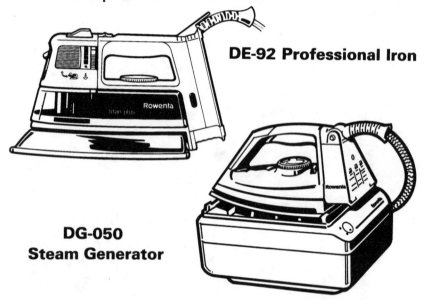

DE-92 Professional Iron

**DG-050
Steam Generator**

Industrial irons are heavier than household irons and have a powerful steam source. Because of their weight, they are best used with a special pressing table like the one I described earlier, or some come with their own tables. Some of the sources in the "Wholesale Buying" chapter of this book carry industrial irons.

Pressing machines contain the pressing unit and the board or bed all in one machine. These presses are particularly suited for fusing interfacing, but they also come with directions for pressing entire garments and their parts. Featured here are two versions of the ElnaPress, the top of the line 3000 and the more economical 1004. As you can see, they would allow you to fuse interfacing to whole sections of garments in one motion as well as press in many different ways. For more infomation call 1-800-848ELNA.

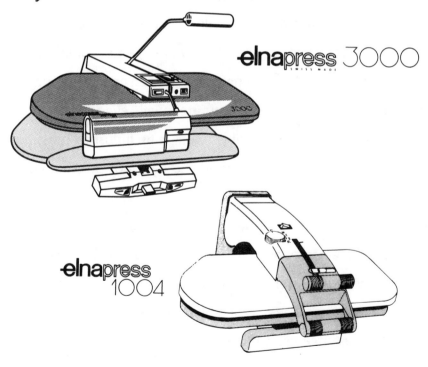

If your business calls for cutting heavy fabric or several layers at a time, you may find an electric rotary cutter useful. An electric cutter will give great relief from back fatigue and sore hands and will increase speed noticeably. See the "Wholesale" chapter for suppliers.

The use of new equipment can greatly increase productivity and save much valuable time and energy, but simply purchasing new equipment will not magically make your business succeed. Feeling accomplished in the use of your home sewing machine will help you feel confident in mastering the use of more powerful and complicated machines. You will only benefit from buying an electric cuttter if you have learned to cut accurately with everyday sewing shears, and you will not be able to utilize an industrial pressing machine if you have not learned the basics of pressing with your home iron.

Most important in the purchase of any equipment is the prestige of the company you buy it from. You will not be able to waste time and money on service policies that do not hold true to their guarantees. Being able to take lessons or having a support system available is also important.

PRICING

Pricing is usually the biggest problem people have whether they are trying to start a sewing business or if they already have one. Either they can't decide how much to charge, or they lack the ability to justify their prices. In this chapter I am going to tell you exactly what to charge for alterations and custom sewing for men and women, how to decide on an hourly rate, how to develop a price list, and how to get the prices you need to stay in business.

If you would like to know how to price a product or craft, refer to the chapter on "Crafts". For pricing bridal alterations and draperies, see the publications at the end of this book. Also, there is an excellent newsletter about the window coverings business called *Sew/What?*, published by Cheryl Strickland, an expert in this field. In addition, Cheryl has a school to learn this profession. For more information call 800-222-1415.

There are basically two ways to charge: by the piece or job, and by the hour. When you charge by the piece or job, you have a set price for a certain task, such as a price for a hem or a price for making a custom made shirt. The advantages to this method are that customers know the exact price in advance and if you increase your speed, you automatically increase your hourly income. The faster you get at doing some task, the more money you will make.

The biggest problem sewers have with this method is in estimating the amount of time it will take them to do a task. You must know your sewing ability, look at what will be involved, and charge a set price. It is generally a bad business practice to add additional charges after quoting a set price so if you take longer than estimated, it is your loss.

When you charge by the hour, you establish an hourly rate and then keep track of your time and charge the customer accordingly when the job is done. This is open-ended and requires that the customer trusts you to keep accurate records.

The advantage to this method is that you will always get paid for all the time you have spent. The disadvantages are that you have to keep track of all your time and you can never make anymore than your hourly rate, even if you increase your speed. Also some customers don't like leaving the price open-ended.

This system necessitates keeping a very accurate record of your work schedule on each separate job. You will log in and out during each work session and tally the total hours after the project is completed. You then multiply the total number of hours times your hourly rate to arrive at the price you will charge the customer. You cannot charge for time spent on things not related to the job, such as answering the phone, eating, taking rest breaks, attending children, or talking to friends. You can add on your time spent for shopping, doing research, fitting, and phone consultations necessary for completing the job. Following is a sample work sheet to help you keep track of your time if you are charging by the hour.

SAMPLE WORK SHEET

Customer _____

Address _____

Phone _____

Garment _____

Measurements _____

Task	Total Time	Task	Total Time

Total Construction Time _____

Hourly Rate _____ x _____ = _____ Total garment cost

Start	Stop	Start	Stop	Start	Stop	Start	Stop	Total

I recommend that you use a combination of the two methods, charging by the piece or job for the majority of your work, and charging by the hour for jobs that are unusual or difficult to figure in advance. When charging by the hour, always try to give the customer an idea up front of how much the job is going to cost. Give an estimate such as, "This will be between $30 and $45." I recommend never charging more than the higher price even if it took longer. Gradually you will become an expert at estimating prices and you will find that any job that you are having trouble estimating will usually take twice as long as you think.

To figure an hourly rate, you decide how much you want to make in a year (your salary) and add your direct costs and overhead expenses to this to get your desired income. Divide this by the number of hours you are going to work in a year and this will give you the hourly rate you must charge.

Direct costs are the amount spent on materials and supplies that go into making a garment. In most home sewing businesses, the customer brings all the materials, but you may have to purchase thread or other notions occasionally.

Overhead expenses are the amount spent on utilities for the business (not on the rest of the house), office supplies, advertising, insurance, maintenance, taxes, licenses, auto expenses, and legal and accounting fees. You may think of other overhead expenses which cause you to spend money to keep your business in operation, or your list may be much smaller.

I am going to give you several examples using different incomes and their corresponding overhead and direct costs so you can see how to figure this. By experimenting with different figures and by deciding what rate you personally feel comfortable with, you will be able to get a clear picture of the hourly rate you should charge.

I am estimating direct costs and using average amounts for overhead expenses based on tax tables from the I.R.S. You may find your expenses are much more or much less, but this will give you a fairly realistic idea.

All of these examples will be based on you working 11 months a year with one month off. They are also based on an average forty-hour work week.

Example 1

Step 1
> **$15,000 Salary** + $3,000 Overhead and Costs =
> $18,000 Earnings Needed

Step 2
> 11 Months x 4 Weeks/Month = 44 Weeks
> 44 Weeks x 40 Hours/ Week = 1760 Hours per Year

Step 3
> $18,000 Earnings Needed ÷ 1760 Hours/ Year =
> **$10.22 Rate per Hour**

Example 2

$20,000 Salary + $6,000 Overhead and Costs =
$26,000 Earnings Needed ÷ 1760 Hours per Year =
$14.77 Rate per Hour

Example 3

$30,000 Salary + $8,000 Overhead and Costs=
$38,000 Earnings Needed ÷ 1760 Hours per Year =
$21.59 Rate per Hour

You can experiment with the number of hours per year or the amount of salary you want to earn to get different examples.

In order to find out if the hourly rate you have chosen is a realistic one, call up an alteration business or drycleaner in your area and ask them how much they charge for an unlined hem in a pair of pants (please note that I believe it is impolite and unfair to call another business and ask for their price list just because you don't know what to charge, but it is reasonable to ask for this basic price when you are just starting out). Let's say the charge is $10.00. This will give you an idea of the going rate in your area, or in other words, what the market will bear. If you can do a hem in an hour, you know that you can make $10 per hour in your area. If you can do two hems in an hour, you can make $20 per hour, etc.

People are always asking me how much they should charge per hour. You should be charging at least $10 per hour. This is an absolute minimum based on nationwide averages and you should be working your way up to at least double this amount. Your hourly rate will be higher in metropolitan than rural areas due to the cost of living.

Incidentally, if you are considering alterations versus custom sewing, the money is in alterations, not in custom sewing. This is not to say that you can't make money in custom sewing, you can. But, the people who do are sewing bridalwear, career clothing, and costumes for entertainers and they are charging the big bucks.

Doing alterations is, in general, more lucrative because alterations are over and done more quickly and you can charge proportionately a much higher rate. Custom sewing is more open-ended with fittings that could go on indefinitely. For custom sewing, the target market is much smaller because you are appealing to an elite group, but with alterations, virtually everyone who wears clothes is a potential customer.

Many people dislike doing alterations, but it is worth your time to learn. Doing alterations is also an excellent way to learn fitting and to increase your sewing skills. I know this is true from experience and that is why I wrote my two books, *Altering Women's Ready-to-Wear* and *Altering Men's Ready-to-Wear*. They are described at the end of this book and they will help you immensely in learning how to fit and to do alterations. Many sewers find that doing alterations and custom sewing are two target markets that compliment each other perfectly.

PRICE LISTS

After you decide on your hourly rate, you then multiply the time it takes you to do a job times your hourly rate and arrive at a price. Price lists take a long time to develop because in the beginning, you don't know how long it will take you to do different tasks and also, the more times you repeat a task, the faster you become. That's why I am including complete price lists for alterations and custom sewing for men and women. If you are sewing for children, you can also use these for estimating prices.

These prices are meant to give you a general idea of that to charge and are definitely not an absolute. They are good nationwide: if you are in a rural area, charge on the low side, and for metropolitan areas, charge on the higher side. Your prices could be lower or higher depending on other factors such as the season, your experience and speed, the length of time you have been in business, and what the market will bear. Most important by far is charging a price that you feel comfortable with and one that allows you to make a living.

Price List for Women's Alterations

I recommend having a minimum charge of $2.00 to $5.00 to prevent people from running in with small tasks and expecting you to do them on the spot. I also charge $5.00 - 10.00 for a rush order. See the "Customer Relations" chapter for instructions on how to conduct a fitting.

PANTS

Hem	shorten or lengthen- unlined	$8.00 - 15.00
	lined	add 4.00
	lengthen and face	add 5.00
	cuffs	add 4.00
	levis	8.00 - 12.00
	with zippers	add 5 - 7.50
	jogging pants	
	with elastic	8.00 - 10.00
	with elastic and zippers	12.00 - 17.50
Waist	in or out through CB seam	7.50 - 10.00
	through sideseams-	
	remove waistband	10.00 - 15.00
	levis- in or out by adding darts	5.00
	by easing onto twill tape	7.50 - 10.00
	through CB waistband	10.00 - 15.00

Seat only	in or out- unlined	$5.00
	lined	7.50
Drop Waistband	unlined	12.00 - 15.00
	lined	12.00 - 15.00
	move zipper	add 5.00 - 7.50
Add Maternity Stretch Panel		10.00 - 12.00 + panel
Waist, Seat, & Stride		
	unlined	15.00
	lined	20.00
Sideseams	in or out- unlined	8.00 - 12.00
	lined	add 5.00
	through pockets	add 10.00 - 15.00
Crotch Adjustment	unlined	7.50
	lined	add 4.00
	crotchpiece	10.00
Tapering Legs	unlined	12.00
	lined	17.50
Replace Zipper	regular pants	9.00 - 15.00
	levis	10.00 - 15.00
Put in Lining		25.00 + fabric

SKIRTS

Hem	shorten or lengthen- unlined	$10.00 first 48"
		add $2 per foot
	lined	add $5 first 48",
		.50 per add. foot
	face	add $1 per foot
	with pleat or vent	add 4.00
	topstitched	add 5.00 -15.00
	wedding gown	25.00 - 50.00
	with train	add 15.00
	shorten from waist	15.00 - 25.00
	move zipper down	add 7.50

Waist and Sides	in or out	same as pants

Sides in Through Hem- unlined		12.00
lined		15.00

Drop Waistband	same as pants

High Hip	7.50

Put in Lining	17.50 + fabric

Replace Zipper	9 - 15.00 + zip

Replace Elastic in Waist

without topstitching	7.50 + elastic
ripping out topstitching	15.00 + elastic

BLOUSES

Narrow Shoulders
by removing sleeve cap	$12.00-20.00
with tucks or darts	4.00 - 6.00

Drop Shoulders   12.00 - 15.00
           drop armhole   add 5.00 - 8.00

Add Darts to Armholes   6.00 - 10.00

Add Darts in Back   6.00

Add Bust Darts   8.00 - 10.00

Sides In or Out- regular seams   7.50 - 10.00
           flat felled seams   add 6.00 - 10.00
           add gussets   8.50 - 10.00

Shortening Sleeves   8.00 - 10.00
           move placket   add 5.00
           from top   12.00 - 20.00
           replace sleeve elastic   5.00 + elastic
Shorten Blouse   6.00 - 10.00
           curved hem   add 3.00

Narrow Collar   10.00 - 12.00
Adjust Neckline   5.00 - 12.00
Change Buttons   .50 each
Make Buttonholes   1.00 each
Make Covered Buttons   2.00 - 5.00 each
Monogram   5.00 - 10.00

DRESSES

For hems, side alterations, and other alterations you don't find here, refer to the blouse price list. For **wedding dresses**, see reference at the end of this book.

Shorten the Bodice (take out blouson)	$15.00
Lengthen the Bodice (usually by adding fabric)	17.50
Reposition Bust Darts	7.50
Adjust for Sway Back	10.00 - 12.00
Take in the Back	7.50
through zipper	12.50
Dowager's Hump	
neck darts in back	5.00 - 7.50
front adjustment	12.00
Hip and Low Shoulder Adjustment	17.50
Shoulder Pads	
add	7.50 + pads
remove	5.00
with armhole adjustment	10.00 - 12.00
Narrow Sleeves	10.00 - 20.00
Let Out Sleeves and Add Gussets	18.50
Change Sleeve Pitch	20.00 - 30.00

JACKETS AND COATS

Sleeves	lengthen or shorten	
	unlined	$6.00 - 10.00
	lined	add 4.00
	face	add 6.00 - 8.00
	with vents	add - 6.00
	shorten from top	25.00
	raincoat- unlined	7.50 - 12.00
	lined	add 4.00
	move tabs	add 3.00
Sideseams	in or out- unlined	10.00 - 12.00
	lined	add 5.00
	into armholes	add 5.00 - 10.00
	through pockets	add 7.50 - 15.00
	add gusset to lining	8.00
Darts	in or out- unlined	5.00
	lined	add 4.00
Take In Center Back Seam- unlined		6.00 - 8.00
	lined	add 4.00
	with vent	add 4.00
Narrow Shoulders- unlined		22.50
	lined	add 7.50
Shoulder Pads- unlined		
	add	6.00 + pads
	remove	4.00
	lined	add 4.00
	armhole adjustment	add 12.00 - 20.00

Hem

Jacket	unlined	$15.00 - 30.00
	lined	add 5.00
	with vent	add 3.00
Coat	first 60" unlined	18.50, $2 each ft.
	lined	add 7.50
	with vent	add 4.00
	lengthen and face	add $10 + facing
Raincoat	unlined	17.50 - 30.00
	lined	add 5.00
	with vent	add 4.00
	lengthen and face	add $10 + facing
Leather	unlined	20.00
	lined	add 7.50
	with vent	add 5.00
	topstitched	add 10.00 - 15.00

Reline	30.00-50.00 +fab.
Add Interlining to Coats	50.00 + fabric
partial interlining	25.00 + fabric

Narrow Lapels	35.00
Widen Lapels	35.00
Add Inside Pocket	8.00 - 12.50

Ski Jacket	replace front zipper	12.00-17.50 +zip.
	replace pocket zipper	10.00 - 12.00+ zip

Price List for Men's Alterations
JACKETS or COATS
(Charge $10.00 - 15.00 for a rush order.)

Sleeves	shorten or lengthen	$8.00 - 17.50
	lengthen and face	add 10.00 - 15.00
	move tabs on raincoat	add 4.00
	narrow	17.50
	correcting sleeve pitch	27.50 - 35.00
Sideseams	in or out- unlined	10.00 - 17.50
	lined	add 5.00
	with double vents	add 6.00
	into armholes- unlined	17.50 - 25.00
	lined	add 5.00
Darts	in or out	9.00 - 12.00
Shoulders	narrowing	35.00 - 45.00
	dropping	37.50 - 50.00
Shorten	unlined	17.50 - 22.50
	lined	22.50 - 40.00
	raincoat	22.50 - 35.00
	leather	30.00 - 50.00
Collars	lowering	9.00 - 17.50
	squaring shoulders	add 10.00
	shortening	25.00 - 35.00

JACKETS or COATS Continued

Lapels

shrinking	$15.00
narrowing	35.00 - 50.00
widening	35.00 - 50.00

Vents

close	10.00
add	12.50

Relining   55.00 + fabric

Add Interlining to Coats- partial   30.00 + fabric
                                 full   50.00 - 65.00 + fab.

Shoulder Pads

add	7.50 each
remove	5.00 each
armhole adjustment	add 15.00 - 20.00

Buttons   resew   1.00 - 2.00 each

Buttonholes

machine	1.50 each
by hand	7.50 each

Ski Jacket

replace front zipper	12.00 - 17.50 + zip.
replace pocket zipper	10.00 - 12.00 + zip.

SHIRTS

Sleeves

shorten	$8.00 - 12.00
move plackets	add 5.00
make short sleeves	7.50 - 10.00

Shorten Shirt 7.50 - 12.00

Darts add 6.00 - 8.00

Sideseams

plain	7.50 - 10.00
flat felled	12.00 - 20.00

Collars

narrowing	10.00 - 12.00
add buttons and buttonholes	5.00 - 7.50
add collar stays	7.50

Emblems or Patches

sew onto sleeves or chest	2.00 each
sew onto pocket	5.00

Monogram 5.00 - 12.50

VESTS

Sideseams

in or out	$10.00 - 15.00
front or back only	12.00 - 17.50

Center Back Seam   9.00 - 12.50

Points Stick Out   7.50

Shrink Lapels   7.50 - 10.00

Removing Back Strap   4.00

Make New Back   20.00 - 30.00 + fab.

Recut Neck and Shoulders   12.50 - 17.50

NECKTIES

Narrowing $7.50 - 12.00

Shortening   6.00 - 10.00

PANTS

Hems	plain bottom	$8.00 - 15.00
	cuffs	add 4.00
	lengthen and face	add 5.00
	heel guards	add 4.00
	levis	10.00 - 15.00
	jogging pants	
	with elastic	8.00 - 10.00
	elastic and zippers	12.00 - 17.50
Waist and Seat		
	in or out	7.50 - 12.00
	seat only	4.00 - 7.50
Waist, Seat, and Stride		10.00 - 17.50
	stride only	7.50 - 10.00
Crotch Adjustment		
	in or out	7.50
	add crotchpieces	10.00 - 15.00
	reshape	6.00
	line	10.00 - 12.00
Sideseams		
	in or out	10.00
	redo pockets	17.50 - 22.50
Dropping the Waistband		22.50 - 27.50
	move watch pocket	add 5.00
	move fly facing	add 5.00

Tapering $12.50 - 17.50

Swing Creases- each leg   10.00 - 12.50

Line

    to knees   15.00-17.50 + fab.

    full   35.00-45.00 + fab.

Replace Zipper   10.00 - 15.00

    levis   12.00 - 15.00

Belt Loops

    add   6.00 - 8.00

    make new   10.00 - 12.50

Waist Snugs   5.00

Pockets

    new half pocket   7.50

    new whole pocket   10.00 - 12.50

    new watch pocket   7.50

    new back bound pocket   10.00 - 12.50

"I CAN'T WAIT MORE THAN 2 WEEKS OR
MY FOOD WILL RUN OUT."

Concerning alterations, there are a few more points to remember. You are not required to work on soiled garments and in some states it is even against the law. You can display a simple sign in your fitting area that says, "Garments Must Be Cleaned Prior to Altering," or, "State Law Requires Garments to be Cleaned Prior to Altering." Ask if it would be convenient for the customer to clean the garment because pressing can set stains in fabric. Some sewers offer to take garments to the cleaners along with their weekly order and charge accordingly. If this becomes an issue, remain calm and be assertive. Your health could be at risk.

Be sure to check garments carefully for stains, rips, missing buttons, torn belt loops, snagged threads, etc., and make mention of these before taking responsibility for garments. Make note on the receipt of such occurrences so you will not be blamed for them later.

Lastly, always examine garments thoroughly before quoting a price. You may not have noticed that the garment is lined, has mitered corners on the sleeves, or has some other hidden detail which adds to sewing time.

If you are going to do alterations for a drycleaner or store, but work in your home, the establishment will always add onto the price you charge, up to as much as doubling it. The great advantage for you is that you don't have to spend time and money advertising or fitting and dealing with customers. On the other hand, you must make it perfectly clear ahead of time that you are not responsible for the fit of the garment, only the quality of the sewing. If you are making the pick-ups and deliveries, it is wise to start out with a policy that there will be an extra charge for extra trips.

Whether you are doing alterations for customers or for establishments, I have found it very helpful to stock standard colors of thread, zippers, elastic, and seam tape, and to include this in my direct costs for tax purposes. See the "Wholesale Buying" chapter for sources that will sell these items to you. In the beginning, it may seem like a box with a dozen spools of thread is a lot, but I guarantee you will use it quicker than you think and the initial investment will be worth it. For unusual colors that would require an extra trip, I tell the customer they can supply the notion or I will be glad to pick it up and charge them for it.

My prices for custom sewing are for labor only. The customer must bring all the materials including fabric, pattern, interfacing, notions, etc. If they are unsure what to get, I tell them to show the fabric store clerk their pattern and ask for advice. If they arrive with a missing or inappropriate item, I offer to purchase the item and charge them, or to trade out a more appropriate item from my stock.

Because I require customers to bring everything, I don't charge extra for an initial consultation, but you should if you are assisting with fabric and pattern selection by showing fabric swatches, looking at pattern books, or sketching designs. If you are going to shop with the customer, always charge at least your regular hourly rate and be sure to start and stop the clock when you leave and arrive home.

My prices include the initial visit, where I take measurements, and two fittings. Depending on how the first fitting went, I will have the garment complete or near completion for the second or final fitting. I explain at the initial visit and at both fittings that I will be glad to make alterations (not style changes) through the last fitting, but there will be an additional charge after that.

Price List for Custom Sewing

WOMEN'S CLOTHING

I give a range in these price lists. If you are in a rural area, charge on the low side; for a metropolitan area, charge on the high side. These prices include labor only. The customer must supply the fabric, lining, interfacing, pattern, notions, etc. Choose a base price for a basic garment and add to it depending on the added details.

Straight Skirt

Base prices

unlined- hems up to 48"	$25 - 50.00
unlined-hems over 48"	3.00 per foot
lined	35 - 60.00

Added prices

pockets	5-12.00 each
vents	5.00 each
topstitching	add 10.00
bias cut	add 10-12.00
plaids	add 10.00
napped fabrics	add 10.00
hand sewn zippers	add 12.00
belt loops	add 10.00
pleats	2.00 each

Broomstick Skirt   35.00 - 70.00

Dress

Base prices

street length	$60 - 90.00
floor length	$75 - 100.00
wedding	$100 - 175

Dresses cont'd.

Added Prices for Dresses

lining	25.00 - 50.00
boning	$12.00 - 25.00
button loop closures	1.00 - 2.00 each
covered buttons	2.00 - 5.00 each
covered belts	15.00 - 45.00
elastic waist casings	10.00
bra cups	12.00
spaghetti straps	12.00 - 20.00
piping	10.00 - 20.00
underdresses or slips	25.00 - 55.00

Check under "**Skirts**" and "**Blouses**" for details you haven't found here. Also, most pattern covers list the circumference of skirt or dress hems so you may not have to measure the pattern for this detail.

Blouse	**Base Price**	$30.00 - 50.00
Tailored Shirt	**Base Price**	40.00 - 50.00

Added Prices for Blouses and Shirts

pleats or tucks	3.00 each
bra stays	3.00
bound buttonholes	3.00 - 7.50 each
extra topstitching	10.00 - 15.00
drawstring	10.00 - 15.00
button down collars	6.00
pockets	7.00 - 15.00 each
monogramming	5.00 - 15.00

Blouses and Shirts cont'd.

Pick a base price that you feel comfortable with from the ranges I have given you for blouses and shirts. A base price is for a garment that really is a simple design. To the base price, add on for any of the details I have listed or any others that you can think of. You will have to estimate a price for those. Some other details might be fabric that is slippery or hard to work with, gathers, ruffles, dress shields, hidden front closures, additions of ribbon or lace, beading or adding pearls, sleeve plackets, yokes, etc. Failure to identify all these details and to charge for them is the major reason people don't get paid enough for their sewing and the reason they get burnt out and resentful.

Pants	**Base Price**	
	unlined	$40.00 - 70.00
	lined	60.00 - 75.00
	fitting muslin	25.00 - 65.00
	maternity pants	add 20.00

Pants are probably the most difficult custom garments because of the fitting. Some sewers make pants only if the customer pays for a fitting muslin in advance. The base prices are for simple pants with no pockets or details. See the added prices on other garments for details found on pants and add them to your base price.

Jackets, Blazers, and Coats

Some dressmakers consider tailoring too difficult and refuse to do it. This is wise, especially if they don't have the skills. Tailoring is much quicker now with fusible interfacings and very professional results are possible. Refer to my book, *Speed Tailoring,* at the end of this book if you are interested in learning about all the new updated ways of doing tailoring. If you are confident to do tailoring, your services will be in great demand. Choose a base price for a basic garment and add to it for extra details.

Base Price for Jackets and Blazers

unlined, fused interfacing	$65 - 95.00
lined, fused interfacing	75 - 125.00
lined, hand pad stitched	200 - 300.00

Base Price for Coats

unlined, fused interfacing	85 - 125.00
lined, fused interfacing	100 - 150.00
lined, hand pad stitched	200 - 350.00

Added Prices

vents on sleeves	7.50
topstitching	12 - 20.00
keyhole buttonholes	
machine	3.00 each
by hand	7.50 each
bound buttonholes	5-7.50 each
matching plaids	10 - 20.00
back vents	7.50 - 10.00
pockets	8 - 12 each
napped fabric	10 - 20.00

The previous prices I have given are for the most common garments that women wear and want custom made. Occasionally you will receive a request for other garments, so I am going to give you some ballpark figures that will help you estimate prices for them. Since these garments are not usually custom made, it is more difficult to estimate a price and I would always like to err on the high side rather than the low side. As I have said before, if there is a job that is difficult to estimate, it will usually take you twice as long as you had planned.

Base Price

Nightgown- flannel or other	$30.00 - 55.00
Pajamas	30.00 - 55.00
Robe	40.00 - 125.00
Maternity	Use base prices for regular garments and add at least $20
Jogging Suit	50.00 - 150.00
Swim Suit	25.00 - 75.00
Aerobic Wear- bodysuit	20.00 - 50.00
Shorts	20.00 - 40.00
Tennis Skirt	20.00 - 40.00
Equestrian	add at least $25 per garment

Price List for Custom Sewing

MEN'S CLOTHING

Because men wear fewer styles of clothing than women and their garments tend to have very similar design details, we usually have a set price for a garment and don't add on for most details that would be considered extra in a pair of pants for women. Such as, most men's pants have a front fly, two side pockets, belt loops, two bound back pockets, and are unlined. These would all be included in a basic pair of pants for men and there are very few added details that are options. But, because men's pants contain more details than women's to begin with, and because most of the details are difficult to sew, their basic pants will be priced higher in general than women's.

Pants   **Base Price** $65 - 125.00

        Added Prices

front lining to knees	20.00
full lining	35.00
crotch lining	12.50
extra or unusual pockets	15.00 each
plaid fabric	20.00

Men's Clothing cont'd.

Shirt	**Base Price**	
	dress or formal	$40.00 - 95.00
	casual or western	40.00 - 90.00

For shirts, it is assumed that the base price includes plackets on the sleeves, pockets, yokes, collar with collar band, flat felled seams, etc. In the dress or formal category, I would charge extra for details like pleats, tucks, or wing collar as in a tuxedo shirt. In the casual (includes Oxford type shirts) or western category, I would charge extra for out-of-the-ordinary pockets or yokes and monogramming. See the women's custom sewing price list for prices on these details.

Vest	**Base Price**	$35.00 - 75.00

Jacket	**Base Price**	
	unlined- fused interfacing	95.00 - 125.00
	lined- fused interfacing	125.00 - 200.00
	lined- hand pad stitched	225.00 - 350.00

Outer Coat	**Base Price**	
	unlined- fused interfacing	125.00 - 200.00
	lined- fused interfacing	150.00 - 200.00
	lined- hand pad stitched	225.00 - 400.00

Necktie	20.00 - 45.00
Pajamas	45.00 - 75.00
Robe	40.00 - 125.00
Jogging Suit	75.00 - 125.00
Swim Suit or Boxers	20.00 - 35.00

Justifying Prices

People in general, women in particular, can have trouble talking about money and asking for money. I have given you an idea of what to charge and have shown you how to develop a price list. Now I would like to show you how to justify your prices to customers.

When I first started my business I prided myself on having all my prices memorized. I thought I was being quite smart, but actually I wasn't. When a customer asks for a price and you quote one from the top of your head this can leave the customer wondering, "Where did that price come from? Is it based on how I look? Does everyone pay the same price?" It leaves the subject open for debate and puts you on the defensive.

After numerous uncomfortable confrontations, I finally wrote out my prices, and I strongly advise you to do the same. Now when customers ask about a price, I pick up the list and show them exactly what they want to know. This takes the pressure off you; the price list did it, not you, and it is hard to debate with a piece of paper.

In addition to making you look more professional, this will let customers know that everyone is charged the same amount and that this is the going rate. You can also post your prices in the room where you see customers or in the changing area. I don't give my price lists to customers because I am always revising them to add new services or to keep up with inflation. Simply type out your price list, and if you can store it on a computer, this will make revision a breeze.

If you quote a price and the customer exclaims, "Wow, that is expensive," or, "That's too much," don't take it personally. Very few people realize just how long and involved many sewing tasks can be, so they do not understand the value of the service you are providing. You will need to educate them in this matter.

Here is where having a printed price list will also help immensely. With alterations, customers can see that there is a base price and you can show them that extra details take extra time so there is an additional charge. You can also explain that even a basic hem on unlined pants requires fitting, marking, ripping, trimming, finishing the edge, sewing, and pressing.

"I JUST WANT A SIMPLE DRESS."

For custom sewing, you can make out a separate task sheet for each garment you are making. Go over it with customers and check off all the tasks that need to be done including those for a base price and all the extra details. Have on hand your price list for custom garments and you can fill in the amounts and add them at the end to get a price for the garment. I have pictured a task sheet for a custom made skirt on the opposite page. You can make up similar ones for other garments.

This will give customers a clear picture of how much time and effort goes into each project, and thus, an appreciation for your services will be developed. After going through this process, you would be amazed at how many people say, "I never realized what went into something like this, it is worth the price," or, "This is a real bargain!"

There may still be customers who will say, "That's just too much for my budget." Thank them and tell them that you hope you can do business with them sometime in the future. This creates a win-win situation. Although you are unable to compromise on your prices, you are leaving the door open for future business when the customer is ready.

Task Sheet for Custom Made Skirt

Customer's name _____

Basic skirt- unlined,
hem circumference up to 48"
Includes two fittings and:

Added details-

__ Taking measurements

__ No. inches over 48"
__ Lining
__ Pockets

__ Pattern alterations

__ Plaid fabric
__ Bias cut

__ Fabric preparation

__ Vents
__ Pleats

__ Fabric layout

__ Hand sewn zipper
__ Belt loops

__ Cutting

__ Covered belt
__ Covered buttons

__ Marking

__ Elastic waist
__ Flat felled seams

__ Staystitching

__ Topstitching
__ Yoke

__ Basting

__ Other

__ Interfacing

__ Fitting

Base price _____

__ Making adjustments

Added details _____

__ Pressing

Total _____

There will always be that customer who says, "That's way too much, I can get it cheaper down the street." Give them a sincere and pleasant smile and reply, "These are the prices I need to charge to stay in business. Of course, you are welcome to shop around." This tells them that you are a professional and you are confident that your prices are fair and your quality high. This is a confidence and credibility booster and will win more customers than it will lose. If they do leave, breathe a sigh of relief. You have lost the type of customer that you didn't want or need anyway!

My normal time for completing jobs is usually one week for alterations and three weeks for custom sewing. For any job, you need to find a time frame that is comfortable for you and fair to the customer. For customers who need their orders in less than your normal time period, try to accommodate them, but always charge extra. Explain by saying, "Yes, I can complete this earlier, but I need to set aside my scheduled work, so there will be a charge for a rush order."

Sewing for friends and relatives can create a problem for you and your business. Often we feel obligated to do work free or under unrealistic time constraints. I solved this problem by giving them a discount and noting it as such on a receipt that I pin to their garments. This shows them that I am a professional, but I am giving them special consideration. You can either take a few dollars off each price or take off a certain percentage like 10 or 20%.

MARY A. ROEHR
Custom Tailoring
500 Saddlerock Circle
Sedona, AZ 86336
520-282-4971

Customer's
Phone no. _____ Date _____

Name *Aunt Sally*

Address _____

SOLD BY	CASH	C.O.D.	CHARGE	ON ACCT.	MDSE. RETD	PAID OUT	

QUAN.	DESCRIPTION	PRICE	AMOUNT	
	Pants - lined			
	Hem		12	00
	Relative's discount	-	2	00
			10	00

If you would like to be able to take credit cards from your customers, you can apply for Visa and Mastercard merchant services through your bank just like you would for a loan. See the chapter on "Financing Your Business" for details on this. Once you establish merchant services for Visa and Mastercard through a bank, you can call American Express at 800-528-5200 and Novus (which includes Discover) at 800-347-2000 and apply to accept these cards. Each credit card service will charge you a percentage which varies from institution to institution. If you get turned down by the bank for some reason, they can usually give you a list of private companies that may accept you, but they will charge a much higher percentage and sometimes an application fee. Every company will have different policies.

When you have too much work, so much that you can't get it done in a reasonable period of time, this is an immediate indication that you need to raise your prices. Keep increasing them until your workload levels off. After this happens, raise your prices about 10% a year to keep up with inflation. This will be gradual enough so as not to be extremely noticeable and will allow you to keep up with the cost of living.

Everyone feels over stressed at some time or another, but there are many, many time and energy savers that can help. I have listed some below. By learning time-saving techniques, you will not only be able to increase your speed and efficiency, you will also be able to increase the quality of your work.

Time and Energy Savers

1. Keep supplies close around the area where you are sewing. Put them nearest the hand that will be using them.

2. Have good lighting so you don't strain to see details. Whenever possible, work on dark colors like navy or black in the daytime when they will be easier to see.

3. Put notions, buttons, or supplies of the same type in storage boxes or drawers together. Label storage areas on the outside.

4. Buy extra bobbins and keep some wound in the basic colors.

5. Keep equipment in top condition by cleaning and oiling machines, sharpening shears, recovering pressing boards, and changing needles regularly.

6. Keep your workroom at a comfortable temperature.

7. Whenever possible, invest in timesaving attachments for your machine like a pleater, gathering foot, or teflon foot.

8. Keep a phone close so you won't have to get up to answer it. Turn on an answering machine when you can't be interrupted and save hand work like hems to do while chatting on the phone with friends.

9. Mark all pieces of a pattern at once. Staystitch all pieces at once. Sew as many seams as possible and then go to the pressing table.

10. Group projects by color to save time changing bobbins and thread.

11. When changing to new thread, tie the new thread to the old thread and pull it through the machine.

12. Get self-threading needles or a magnifying attachment for your machine.

13. Do difficult work early when you're fresh.

14. Make a work plan or keep a list of what you want to accomplish each day, week, or month.

15. Purchase zippers, thread, elastic, and hem tape in basic colors to keep on hand.

16. Changing to a new project when you are fatigued or stymied will refresh you.

17. Keep your work area pleasant. Fill a bulletin board with stimulating and up-to-date ideas. Treat yourself to a bouquet of flowers, a plant, or a dried arrangement.

18. Eat regular meals, drink enough liquids, and take breaks.

19. Watch T.V. or videotapes and listen to the radio or a cassette while doing boring tasks.

20. Wear comfortable and attractive clothing even though you are just around the house. Fixing your hair or putting on make-up will give you a quick pick-me-up.

21. Keep a bookshelf close with good references.

22. Pin instead of baste, use fewer pins, machine baste, fuse baste, or sew directly with no pins or basting, depending on your increased skill.

23. Throw your old small pins away and buy ones with glass or plastic ends. They are easier to pick up, you only need half as many because they are twice as long, and they won't get lost in the carpet.

24. Return customers' leftover fabric scraps, notions, and patterns. This will cut down on clutter in your work area and free you from the guilt of not putting all your leftovers to use.

25. Keep scratch pad and pencil handy for ideas, notes, or phone messages.

26. Read and take classes constantly to learn new tips.

Don't expect to speed up instantly. Start on one or two ideas and gradually they will become second nature. There will always be a new gadget or machine that can make your job easier. Talk to others and take seminars or workshops to keep updated. I have been in business for more than 20 years but I still read books and take classes whenever I can, even if they aren't directly related to my specific niche. I feel that if I learn one helpful tip it was worth my time. Seeing how others do things can also help you develop your own techniques or enable you to see a new slant on some problem you've had. Most important, try consciously to work faster all the time. An attitude change can be your biggest asset.

CONTRACTING, CONSIGNMENT, and CRAFTS

Contracting

As your business grows, you may think about hiring help. In a home-based business, hiring employees requires extra space and a lot of extra bookkeeping concerning payroll and income and social security taxes. An alternative is to hire independent contractors.

Under this system you "farm out" work to other people and then pay them when they complete it. The I.R.S. has specific guidelines which distinguish an independent contractor from an employee and these are available to you. Basically, an independent contractor must work in their own home, at their own pace, with skills they already possess, and may not be under the control of anyone else while they are doing so. They receive payment from you for the work they have done and are responsible for paying their own income and social security taxes.

In large cities, independent contractors advertise or sometimes run ads in the yellow pages. You may need to run an ad yourself to find them. One overworked seamstress ran a small ad in the classified section of her paper for "people who want to make money sewing in their homes," and received 30 responses.

Before doing business with independent contractors, you must interview them extensively as to their abilities, preferences, experience, and what type of machines they own. You can ask to see some work they have done, have them make a sample, or ask for references. You will need to explain in detail what it is that you need done and arrive at a price that is acceptable to you both. Also, decide in advance who will do pick up or delivery. It is best to state this all in a written contract for each job. You can make your own stylized contract and run copies or purchase blank forms at an office supply store (I have used Purchase Order forms).

On the contract, always list your name, address, and phone, and those of the independent contractor's. Include a detailed description of the job, a list of the materials or components, a date for completion, the payment, and who will be responsible for pick-up and delivery. Always have the independent contractor sign the contract and give them a copy.

It is best to call the contractor about halfway through the time period of the contract to see if there are any problems and to check on the date of completion. Some people have trouble meeting deadlines or pacing themselves and you may need to encourage them in a friendly but firm manner. You will save yourself a lot of trouble if you enforce due dates from the beginning. You must also uphold your end of the bargain by paying upon completion of the job.

Consignment

Placing your garments, products, or crafts in a consignment shop can be a way to make money, get name recognition, or test the market for future production and sales. You can usually find consignment shops in the Yellow Pages under that heading, even in most small towns. They will want to see what you are selling, usually by appointment, so be prepared to present both your product and yourself as professionally as possible.

Consignment shops usually ask how much you want for the product and then will mark it up around 100% (they will double the price) to sell it. This can be a strong consideration, especially if you have invested a lot of time and/or materials in the item.

Any reputable consignment shop will have a contract for you to sign which states the date, what you are selling, the price and percentage you will receive, the length of time the goods will be on consignment, and a markdown schedule. Most shops carry items for 30 to 90 days and mark them down by some percentage once a month. Many will give you the option of taking merchandise instead of cash. If the shop does not have a contract, I highly recommend that you make up your own for them to sign.

Crafts

Making and selling crafts can be a lucrative business if you have a unique product, price it right, and market it successfully. Many, many books have been written on this subject and I urge you to do your research by looking under the heading of "crafts" at the library. I am going to give some basic information and resources to help you get started.

First of all, I would like to show you a basic business equation for pricing a craft. This will help you decide if making and selling an item is even feasible. Take the cost of the materials (whatever it took to make the craft) and multiply that figure by five. This will give you the selling price of the craft. For instance, let's say you have made a Christmas tree skirt. Your neighbor sees it and wants to buy one. You wonder, "Could I make money selling these?" Multiply the cost of your materials (fabric, thread, sequins, etc.) by five and this gives you the price you should charge for the tree skirt. Then ask yourself, "Would anyone pay that for a tree skirt?" If the price seems exorbitant and you know no one would ever pay that price for it, don't even try to produce them. But, if the price seems reasonable, make some more, about a dozen or so, and try to sell them. This will be your test market and will give you an idea of how they will sell. It will also save you the disappointment of making up large quantities and then not being able to sell them.

You will also need to ask yourself if this price pays for the time spent in making the item. Some crafts are cheap to produce from a materials standpoint, but not from a labor standpoint. If people seem to love the product but don't buy because the price is too high, you may be able to find cheaper sources for supplies or a new faster method of production. Buying materials wholesale will probably be a necessity and this can be difficult for small businesses. The "Wholesale Buying" chapter of this book lists some excellent sources geared to small businesses. Also, Offinger Management at P.O. Box 2188, Zanesville, Ohio, 43702, 614-452-4541 puts on trade shows across the country called Professional Crafters Trade Shows where craft producers can shop for materials to make all kinds of crafts.

Marketing crafts can be done in numerous ways including traditional advertising, in consignment shops, at consumer shows, and through home parties, catalogs, and stores. I have previously discussed advertising and consignment. Many crafters have had success making a large quantity of crafts and hosting an open house sale for several days a year. This works particularly well for Christmas or holiday items.

Craft shows, where sellers rent a booth and sell their wares directly to consumers, are probably where the greatest quantity of crafts are sold. These are extremely popular all over the country and many are now "juried" meaning that the items to be sold must be judged and approved beforehand. Various craft magazines advertise regional and national consumer craft shows. The magazine, *Neighbors & Friends*, P.O. Box 294402, Lewisville, Texas, 75029, 214-539-1073, lists many of them.

If you want to sell your crafts to stores or catalogs, two

organizations that sponsor trade shows are **Hobby Industry Association (HIA)/Mid-Atlantic Craft & Hobby Association (MATCH), 319 East 54th Street, Elmwood Park, New Jersey, 07407, 201-794-1133,** and **Association of Crafts & Creative Industries (ACCI), 1100-H, Brandywine Blvd., Zanesville, Ohio, 43702, 614-452-4541.**

At these shows you would be exhibiting to buyers for stores and catalogs. They will expect to pay wholesale (50% of retail) or distributor prices (usually about 35% of retail) depending on the quantity ordered. This can be the ultimate situation for a crafter, or it can be a nightmare if you are not prepared to produce and deliver large orders on time. You can also contact these buyers directly by calling the store or catalog and asking for the name of the buyer. When you reach the buyer, be prepared to offer samples and/or photographs, promotional literature about your product, and to answer questions about quantity orders and shipping dates.

If the company decides to place an order, you may have to do special packaging, guarantee the price for a year or more, or even help pay for display fixtures to hold your craft. Be aware that most companies do not pay for 30 to 60 days after ordering, and may ask to return unsold goods.

WHOLESALE BUYING

Trying to buy wholesale can be a "Catch 22" for small businesses because we have a great need to buy wholesale in order to succeed, but many suppliers require large minimum orders or have other stipulations that exclude us. I am going to give you a list of companies who cater to small businesses, but first, for future reference, I am going to explain how most wholesale buying is done.

Most wholesalers will want to see either a business license and/or a resale tax number (see the chapters on "Setting Up Shop" and "Taxes" for these), and they will probably want you to fill out a credit application to establish an account. This will enable you to place orders with the company and be billed later. Usually payment is due in 30 days. You might be asked to submit a financial statement along with the credit application. The reason this doesn't work for most new businesses is that the credit applications (see next page) usually require us to list business references or other supppliers that we won't have if we're just starting out.

CREDIT
APPLICATION

APPLICANT: BUSINESS OR CORPORATE NAME

| | APPLICATION DATE |

BUSINESS STREET ADDRESS

BILLING ADDRESS OR P.O. BOX

BUSINESS TELEPHONE #	YEARS BUSINESS WAS ESTABLISHED	NUMBER OF EMPLOYEES	APPROXIMATE NET WORTH OF BUSIN.	BUS. BUILDING/ OWNED OR RENTEI

WE ARE ENGAGED IN THE BUSINESS OF

TYPE OF BUSINESS: SOLE PROPRIETOR
PARTNERSHIP CORPORATION

OWNERS (IF APPLICANT IS A SOLE PROPRIETORSHIP OR PARTNERSHIP) OFFICERS (IF A CORPORATION)

NAME	TITLE	HOME ADDRESS	HOME PHONE #
NAME	TITLE	HOME ADDRESS	HOME PHONE #
NAME	TITLE	HOME ADDRESS	HOME PHONE #

BANK OR SAVINGS AND LOAN ASSOCIATION:

NAME	BRANCH TELEPHONE #	ACCOUNT#	TYPE OF ACCOUNT

APPLICANT'S PRINCIPAL SUPPLIERS ARE (LIST AT LEAST THREE)

NAME	ADDRESS	AMOUNT OWING

HAS APPLICANT OR ANY OF ITS OFFICERS, PRINCIPALS, PARTNERS, OFFICERS, OR DIRECTORS EVER FILED A VOLUNTARY PETITION IN BANKRUPTCY, BEEN ADJUDGED BANKRUPT, OR MADE AN ASSIGNMENT FOR THE BENEFIT OF CREDITORS?
WRITE ANSWER YES OR NO

ARE TAXES OWED BY APPLICANT TO ANY TAXING AUTHORITY CURRENT?	HAS A TAX LIEN OR CIVIL SUIT BEEN FILED AGAINST APPLICANT OI ANY OF ITS OWNERS, PRINCIPALS, PARTNERS, OFFICERS, OP DIRECTORS WITHIN THE PAST SIX YEARS?

APPLICANT: PLEASE COMPLETE AND SIGN REVERSE SIDE OF THIS FORM

OFFICIAL USE:

-122-

LISTED BELOW, OR ATTACHED, IS APPLICANT'S COMPLETE FINANCIAL STATEMENT AS OF _____ ENTER DATE HERE
UPON WHICH FABRIC WHOLESALERS, INC. MAY RELY FOR THE PURPOSE OF ESTABLISHING CREDIT:

CURRENT ASSETS:

CURRENT LIABILITIES:

CASH ON HAND.....................$_____
CASH IN BANK..................... _____
ACCOUNTS RECEIVABLE:CURRENT...... _____
              WORK IN PROGRESS.. _____
              RETENTION .... _____
NOTES RECEIVABLE .... _____
MERCHANDISE INVENTORY............ _____
OTHER (DESCRIBE)_____   _____

TOTAL CURRENT ASSETS .... $_____

ACCOUNTS PAYABLE.......$_____
CONTRACTS PAYABLE...... _____
TAXES PAYABLE.......... _____
OTHEP (DESCRIBE)....... _____
_____   _____
_____   _____
_____   _____

TOTAL CURRENT LIABILITY.$_____

FIXED ASSETS:

LONG TERM LIABILITY:

REAL ESTATE_____ $_____
OTHER (DESCRIBE) _____ _____
TOOLS AND MACHINERY........... _____
AUTOMOTIVE EQUIPMENT.......... _____
FURNITURE AND FIXTURES........ _____

TOTAL FIXED ASSETS............ $_____

NOTES PAYABLE..........$_____
MORTGAGES PAYABLE...... _____
  (MONTHLY PAYMENT$_____)
LOAN FROM OFFICERS..... _____
OTHEP (DESCRIBE)_____ _____
_____   _____

TOTAL LONG TEPM LIABILITIES
                        $_____

OTHER ASSETS

TOTAL LIABILITIES.....$_____
NET WORTH OR
    CAPITOL   _____
    SURPLUS$_____
    STOCK $_____

LOANS AND ADVANCES TO OFFICERS
    AND EMPLOYEES............... $_____
OTHER (DESCRIBE)_____ _____
TOTAL OTHER ASSETS............. $_____

TOTAL ASSETS.................. $_____

TOTAL LIABILITIES
& NET WORTH ....$_____

STATEMENT OF PROFIT AND LOSS FROM _____ 19____, TO _____ 19____

SALES $_____.
GROSS PROFIT $_____
TOTAL OPERATING EXPENSE _____
NET PROFIT OR (LOSS) $_____

APPLICANT AUTHORIZED FABRIC WHOLESALERS, INC TO OBTAIN CREDIT AND FINANCIAL INFORMATION
CONCERNING THE APPLICANT AT ANY TIME AND FROM ANY SOURCE.

EXECUTED AT _____, ON THE _____DAY OF _____, 19_____

_____   _____
APPLICANT'S SOCIAL SECURITY NO.   NAME OF APPLICANT

Following is a list of suppliers who give excellent service to small businesses. I have listed their requirements. Please do not abuse their policies by asking for smaller minimums or other deals. These companies have already gone above and beyond what most wholesalers do.

Most of these companies supply some or all of the following: fabric, notions of all kinds, craft supplies, trims, tailoring supplies, pressing equipment, machines, scissors, cutting equipment, needles, books, work tables, drapery supplies, dry cleaning supplies, marking aids, business forms, and more. Some also carry hard-to-find industrial machines.

Fabric Depot
700 S.E. 122nd Ave., Portland, OR., 97223
800-392-3376
Visa, Mastercard, Discover
They sell by the full bolt or full box at 40 - 50% off, do not require a license or tax number, and do not charge sales tax.

Oregon Tailor Supply
2123A S.E. Division, Portland, OR., 97202
800-678-2457
Visa and Mastercard
They require a business name or license, have a $5.00 minimum order, and do not charge sales tax.

Atlanta Thread & Supply Co.
695 Red Oak Rd., Stockbridge, GA., 30281
800-847-1001
Visa, Mastercard, Discover, American Express
They do not require a license or tax number and there is no minimum order.

SouthStar Supply Co.
P.O. Box 90147, Nashville, TN., 37209
615-353-7000
Visa, Mastercard, American Express
No minimum order.

B & G Lieberman
2420 Distribution St., Charlotte, N.C., 28203
704-376-0717, Fax 704-333-1676
Visa, Mastercard, Discover
They do not require a license or tax number, minimum order $40.00.

S.C.S.
9631 N.E. Colfax St., Portland, OR., 97220
800-542-4727
Visa, Mastercard, Discover, American Express
They do not require a license or tax number and they sell at 15% over wholesale.

David Kaplan & Co., Inc.
530 East Santa Rosa Drive, DesPlaines. IL., 60018
800-852-3201
They are not set up for credit cards, but take C.O.D. orders, do not require business license or tax number.

CUSTOMER RELATIONS

One of the most common questions I get from people who want to start sewing businesses is, "What if I screw something up?" Believe it or not, in more than 20 years I have never ruined a project and I have never talked to anyone who has.

I have done some bleeps and blunders though. The smallest have been the times I cut garments off on the actual hemline and didn't leave a hem to fold up (I say "garments" because I have done it more than once). In these situations I have always been able to add facings and salvage the jobs.

My only major blunder occurred when a woman brought me a piece of navy wool to make a skirt. We had both assumed which was the right side and when she came for the first fitting, we found we had assumed differently. Obviously, if you couldn't tell which was the right side (and I guarantee I had a much better idea than she did), it really didn't matter which side was used. I didn't charge her for the skirt and I'm sure she wore it. I had learned a valuable lesson for the future.

If you feel your skills may not be up to par, or if you are just fearful in general, you can do what I have always done. I decided early in my business that I would not accept any job that made me uncomfortable or that I couldn't afford to reimburse the customer for. I feel this policy has saved me a lot of headaches and worry and has contributed to the success of my business.

I have also learned that the way in which you deal with customers will determine if you are running your business or if it is running you. In other words, you must be in control during all business transactions. Along with your responsibility to do top quality work, you will need to "train" customers to be on time for appointments, effectively handle complaints, and stimulate repeat business.

Let's start from the beginning. Your first contact with a customer may be on the telephone, so always answer in a businesslike way. You may decide to get a separate phone line for your business and then you can answer with your business name. In general, "Good morning," or, "Good afternoon. How can I help you?", would be appropriate. If the customer addresses you incorrectly, correct your name and spell it if necessary. Have a pad of paper by the phone so you can jot down the customer's name and take notes. Ask how they heard about your business so you will be able to judge the effectiveness of your advertising and promotion.

If you have only one phone line, it is very important to have family members understand the necessity of good phone manners. Children in particular, will need to be educated to take and give messages accurately. Help them by practicing what you would like them to say and have a pencil and paper ready at all extensions for messages.

Before quoting any prices, question customers thoroughly about the jobs they want done. Gather as many details as possible in order to get an accurate picture of what they expect. It is a good idea to give only an estimate on the phone until you can see the project. Whether you give an estimate or quote a direct price, write it down next to their name and date it. It is not uncommon for customers to wait several weeks or months after the initial phone call to have the work done.

If you are going to see customers by appointment only, say so from the beginning. You will be communicating the fact

"I THINK YOU FINALLY GOT A CUSTOMER!"

that you have other customers, but each will receive your exclusive attention at their allotted time. Tell customers what to bring such as the proper shoes and undergarments that will be worn with the garment. Give specific directions to your home and mention any special parking or entrance accommodations. Be sure to get the customer's telephone number. Repeat the appointment time and date and don't forget a "thank you."

Included in the subject of telephone etiquette is the option of whether or not to use an answering service or machine. The biggest argument in favor of either is that your chances of missing potential business calls will be decreased. The biggest negative of a machine is that some people dislike leaving messages on recorders. In this case, live answering services are sometimes more popular. If you do decide to use an answering service or machine, always return calls promptly.

Your second contact with a customer will be a fitting or first appointment. Never underestimate the power of a first impression. Even without speaking, many facts can be communicated such as approximate age, nationality, occupation, interests, religion, economic status, and marital status. By simple body language, we convey personality characteristics like patience, assertiveness, shyness, friendliness, cautiousness, and confidence. By observing people's actions, we can tell if they are willing to participate, if they are distracted, or if they are embarrassed.

Because of this, always try to make the most of a first impression. Since you are working in the clothing profession, the way you dress will be of utmost importance. This does not mean that you have to have an extensive high-fashion wardrobe, but your ability to sew and fit others should be evident by the way you dress. Your clothing should be clean, becoming, and comfortable. A few well-fitting classic styles will go a lot farther than a closet full of trendy impulse items.

Try to convey a courteous, but businesslike manner with your speech and gestures. Put customers at ease by greeting them pleasantly, calling them by name, and introducing yourself. Show them where to sit, stand, change clothes, place their belongings, or wait.

When conducting a fitting, you will need to constantly question and instruct customers. Position them in front of the mirror and ask them to stand on both feet and to look forward.

Explain that turning or looking down will change how the garment falls and it will affect the fit. For customers who appear nervous or embarrassed, you can "break the ice" by firmly touching their shoulders while positioning them in front of the mirror. Explain what you are doing as you go by saying, "I will pin the sides," "I'll mark the hem now," or, "Stand still and I will go around you."

While you are doing the fitting, ask customers their preferences by saying, "How does that look?", "Do you like it tighter?", "Does it feel too loose?", or "Shall I make it shorter?" Try to use socially acceptable terms when referring to parts of the body such as hips instead of rear end, apex or point of the bust instead of nipple, and bust instead of boobs. Refer to an extra roll of fat as extra width or say, "Your are fuller here." Replace skinny with slender or thin. Don't try to avoid a handicap or deformity, because that may be the reason the customer needs your help. On the other hand, try not to be shocked or to stare. Treat a handicap or deformity as part of the whole by addressing the problem and trying to solve it.

Reserve your opinion until you are asked for it. Your job is to please customers. Hopefully they will seek your professional advice, but ultimately the final decision will be theirs. If the customer has a strong preference for a style or fit that is different from yours, you will be much better off catering to the customer's choice unless you truly feel it is an alteration that just won't work, an unflattering style, or a poor combination of fabric and pattern. Try to make diplomatic statements like, "I could take in the pants this much but it would cause the pockets to pull. Could you stand them a bit looser?", or, "I really feel your fabric would not drape well in this style. Could I show you some designs that might work better?" Your suggestions will be much more welcome if customers know you are concerned with their happiness.

If the customer absolutely will not take your advice on a matter you feel strongly about, you can always say, "I'm sorry, but I don't feel confident that this will turn out the way you want, so I'd rather not do it," and explain the reasons why. If you are pressed, you can politely but firmly refuse again or you can opt to go ahead with the project by saying, "All right, I will do my best but I cannot be responsible for the fit. If you would like me to proceed, I'll write that on the ticket for you to sign."

"I HAVE A FIGURE LIKE AN HOURGLASS-
TIME JUST STOPPED IN THE WRONG PLACES!"

During the meeting, always record as many details as possible on the receipt pad such as the customer's name, address, and phone number. Describe the garment in writing, such as "Navy pleated wool skirt- unlined." Record what work is to be done, and note special details like "hand hemmed" or "topstitched." Date the receipt and state your terms for payment so they are understood from the beginning. If you collect a down payment, calculate the balance. For custom garments, refer to the task sheet in the "Pricing" chapter.

When the meeting or fitting is over, hang garments neatly rather than leaving them on the floor or draped over furniture. For custom or other work, gather materials together and put them in a bag or box so nothing gets lost. Give customers a time estimate for completion or set up the next appointment. Always end with a big "thank you!"

No matter how reputable the business, an occasional customer complaint is unavoidable. Following are some tips that will help in this area:

*Always do the best possible work. If you have fulfilled your end of the bargain, there will be very few reasons for complaints.

*Keep accurate records of everything. You may need to refer back to them. Describe in detail the specifications for the job and make note of and date any changes that the customer may make over the phone.

*At your first meeting specify time limits for redos and charges for the same if there are any. For instance, you will make changes through the last fitting and there will be a charge after that. Decide on your return policies and write them on the receipt.

*Always be professional and businesslike with customers no matter how friendly you become. Give receipts for everything, even for work redone or done free.

*Never admit guilt on the phone. First of all, if you have done your best, there will be a very slim chance that the complaint is legitimate. Secondly you have no control over what happens to garments or products after they leave your home, so reserve comment until you see the item. Say you are sorry there is a problem and ask when a convenient time would be to get together.

*Always remain calm, even if the customer isn't. If the complaint turns out to be a legitimate one, fix it cheerfully. Examples of illegitimate complaints would be wanting a style change after explicitly requesting the one they have, wanting a hem changed after not bringing the proper shoes for the fitting, wanting free alterations after gaining or losing weight, or wanting you to adjust window treatments when you were working from measurements taken by the customer.

*If the customer is wrong, try not to be accusing or sarcastic. By referring to the receipt or business contract, you should easily be able to find who is in error without pointing a finger. Most problems arise from misunderstandings and can be solved without ill feelings.

In general, when dealing with customers, present yourself as a professional. Keep your personal life and theirs out of the conversation and try to keep the subject on business or go back to it as soon as possible. When customers ramble on, sometimes it is necessary to interrupt by saying, "Excuse me, but we really need to move along," and then proceed.

It is easy to become isolated if you're working alone in your home. Following are several great organizations for support, networking, and general sewing news.

Professional Association of Custom Clothiers (PACC), P.O. Box 8071, Medford, OR., 97504, 503-772-4119.

American Sewing Guild (ASG), P.O. Box 8476, Medford, OR., 97504, 503-772-4059, Fax 503-770-7041.

Professional Sewing Association, Inc. (PSA), 43 Eswin St., Cincinnati, OH., 45218, 513-230-5368.

Lastly, there have been many, many times, especially during the early years of my business, when I got discouraged and wanted to quit. After awhile I realized that this happened because I had become a workaholic. I wasn't eating properly, I was staying up late (or all night) to finish work, and I never scheduled a break or free time. Now I know I need to take a vacation at least every six months and I need to have breaks and free time just like people who have "regular" jobs. I'm much happier and more prosperous because I'm in control of my life and my business. You can be too. I wish you the best of luck in your sewing endeavors!

ALTERING WOMEN'S READY-TO-WEAR is 200 pages and over 300 illustrations. Follow easy directions for altering pants, skirts, blouses, dresses, jackets, coats, and miscellaneous clothing. It shows how to fit, mark, rip, press, and deal with customer complaints. A complete price list is included as well as a comprehensive index. Whether you want to alter your own clothing, or if you do alterations for others, finally all of your questions will be answered! $19.95

ALTERING MEN'S READY-TO-WEAR is over 150 pages with hundreds of illustrations. Drawings show how to identify the problem and what to do to correct it for pants, shirts, vests, neckties, jackets, and coats. It includes marking, ripping, sewing, hand stitches, and pressing. A complete price list tells you what to charge if you want to sew for others. If you have wanted to learn how to alter men's clothing, now is the time to start! $17.95

THESE BOOKS ARE A MUST FOR ANYONE WHO SEWS!

HOW TO ALTER A BRIDAL GOWN was written by Susan Ormond who has over 15 years experience in the alteration and custom design of bridal and formalwear. Completely illustrated, this book has clear instructions on how to alter almost any kind of bridal gown in almost anyway you can think of. It also includes fitting the gown, hand beading, adding a bustle, cleaning and pressing, preserving the gown, supply sources, and much, much more. Susan also gives tips for billing customers and includes an average price list for the alterations. You can make a lot of money altering bridal gowns, and this is THE book that shows you how to do it! $12.95

SPEED TAILORING is a completely illustrated manual that explains in a step-by-step way how to construct a woman's jacket or winter coat using the fastest and most up-to-date methods. It includes complete instructions on how to use fusible interfacing, machine shoulder pad application, professional collar and lapel placement (as is done in ready-to-wear), cutting, marking, sewing the lining in on the machine, finishing, pressing, pockets, buttonholes, and more. In her book, Mary writes in the same clear and forthright manner that she uses in her speed tailoring classes. Whether you are a novice or have done tailoring before, you can do it in a fraction of the time and get couture results! $14.95

PRESSING TO PERFECTION is the 1-hour companion video to **SPEED TAILORING**. In it, Mary shows how tailors really construct and press a jacket or coat. She discusses pressing equipment and the principles of pressing, the difference between a hard press and a soft press, and chestpiece and twill tape application. See close-up how to apply fusible interfacing, how to use a tailor's ham, sleeve board, clapper, and much more. This is your chance to see many of the techniques Mary learned in her apprenticeship- this is the real thing! $24.95

MEASURING
 *What to measure
 *Key error- free guidelines
 *Sample measuring form

DETERMINING FINISHED SIZES
 *Recommended mounting positions
 *Crucial allowances

CALCULATING YARDAGE
 *The yardage formula
 *Allowances for each specific
  treatment
 *Pattern repeats
 *Wide fabrics

According to internationally acclaimed author and speaker, Cheryl Strickland, "Every penny counts in the success of your business!" That's why she tells in concise and easy-to-follow instructions how to master the techniques for measuring, determining finished sizes, and calculating yardages. **A PRACTICAL GUIDE TO SOFT WINDOW COVERINGS** also includes over 100 detailed illustrations and 45 Sample Problems to help reinforce your new skills. At last, the window coverings book you've been looking for! $19.95

PRICE SURVEY OF WINDOW COVERING PROFESSIONALS is a very detailed nationwide survey of what window covering professionals charge. It gives retail and wholesale prices for over 100 window treatment styles from simple pleated draperies to shirred, corded headboards. Responses were tabulated and the results are listed in ranges as well as averages. $5.00

ANNOUNCING MY NEW BOOK

All the cartoons in this book came from **SEW HILARIOUS**, sewing's first cartoon book. I have been working on this book for 10 years and many of the characters and situations are real or really happened to me, my friends, and students. Enjoy 64 pages of ribtickling cartoons about "Learning to Sew," "Sewing for Others," "Sewing as Therapy," "Sewing Getaways," and more. The last chapter, "The Life of a Fabriholic," ties this humorous yarn together. At last, a cartoon book just for sewers- a great gift for your sewing buddies! $9.95